S0-BKK-179

All Roads Lead Somewhere

A Journey Through the Apostles' Creed

All Roads Lead Somewhere

A Journey Through the Apostles' Creed

Stefano Piva

Guardian BOOKS

Belleville, Ontario, Canada

All Roads Lead Somewhere
Copyright © 2004, Stefano Piva

All Rights Reserved. No part of this publication may be reproduced, stored in a retrieval system or transmitted in any form or by any means—electronic, mechanical, photocopy, recording or any other—except for brief quotations in printed reviews, without the prior permission of the author.

First Printing January 2004
Second Printing November 2011

Scripture quotations marked (NLT) are taken from *The Holy Bible, New Living Translation.* Copyright © 1996. Used by permission of Tyndale House Publishers, Inc., Wheaton, IL 60187. All rights reserved.

National Library of Canada Cataloguing in Publication
Piva, Stefano, 1973-
   All roads lead somewhere : a journey through the Apostles' Creed /
Stefano Piva.
Includes bibliographical references.
ISBN 1-55306-712-6   1. Apostles' Creed. I. Title.
BT993.3.P48 2003   238'.11   C2003-905934-0

For more information or
to order additional copies, please contact:
Stefano Piva
8995 Watson Court,
Delta, British Columbia, Canada V4C 8A1
Email: SPiva@BethanyBaptist.bc.ca

Guardian Books is an imprint of *Essence Publishing,* a Christian Book Publisher dedicated to furthering the work of Christ through the written word. For more information, contact:
20 Hanna Court, Belleville, Ontario, Canada K8P 5J2.
Phone: 1-800-238-6376 • Fax: (613) 962-3055.
E-mail: info@essence-publishing.com
Web site: www.essence-publishing.com

table of contents

acknowledgements

I would like to thank all those who have had a part in *continually* introducing me to the heights, depths, lengths, and widths of the Triune God who loves me. I'm still only scratching the surface—aren't we glad we have all of eternity!

I would also like to say thanks to Karen Giebelhaus, who read over these chapters and provided me with helpful suggestions, editing, and points of clarification. Also, thanks to the people of Greenfield Baptist Church, who have sat under my teaching, asked great questions, given me beneficial feedback, striven to live the life, and who have simply been a great church community that has made their pastor feel very loved and supported.

I would also especially like to thank my wife Nancy. She has given me countless hours of patient listening as I have wrestled through trying to understand God more deeply and how best to teach others about him. She also has proofread, edited, made suggestions, and sacrificed a number of evenings in order to allow me to finish this book. I dedicate this project to her. May this little resource be used to the furtherance of the building up of Christ's Kingdom.

introduction

Everyone believes. Everyone has faith. Everyone is religious. For some people, this may come as a shock. For instance, the atheistic philosopher Bertrand Russell claimed there was no outside standard of right and wrong, but that each individual was his or her own arbiter of value.[1] Although Russell prided himself on not being religious, we find here a personal religious ideology.

Speaking of "the modern era," another writer said, "No previous age has been so firmly convinced of the idea that this material world is all there is."

I remember a conversation with a German exchange student where this ideology came out very strongly. He took the position that faith in something was the same as naïve superstition. He went

---

[1] See Bertrand Russell, *Why I Am Not a Christian* (New York, NY: Touchstone, 1957).

on to say he didn't have a faith, but accepted only what was *rational* and *scientific*. When I asked him to explain to me where the first thing that ever existed came from, he answered by saying there always was *something*. When I asked him how he *knew* this, and what evidence he had to prove it, he said that he just knew. I didn't find his answer scientific or rational.

We all believe things. In fact, to be human is to think and to hold to a set of beliefs. Even saying we *don't* believe in anything is a statement about what we believe. G.K. Chesterton wrote:

> The human brain is a machine for coming to conclusions; if it cannot come to conclusions it is rusty.... When a person drops one doctrine after another, declining to tie themselves to a system, and thinking they have outgrown definitions, they sit as God, holding no form of creed but contemplating all, then by that very process they sink backwards into the vagueness of animals and the unconsciousness of the grass. Trees have no dogmas.... The truth is the modern world is filled with people who hold dogmas so strongly that they do not even know they do so.[2]

So the question arises—"If everyone believes something, how do we know what we *should* believe?" For, as the title of this book states, all roads lead somewhere—some lead you off a cliff, some lead you to a dead end, some lead to places you would never want to go, and some lead you *closer* to life's meaning; but, in the midst of this maze of pathways, there is a road that leads to the one who is meaning. With the Apostles' Creed as our map, let's see where this journey takes us.

Our Purpose

The purpose of this book is to help you wrestle with your questions and help you come to some conclusions. To do this, we are

---

[2] G.K. Chesterton, *Heretics/Orthodoxy* (Nashville, TN: Nelson, 2000) p. 151–153.

going to look at the claims of Christianity as presented in the Apostles' Creed. At the end of this study, you may come to the conclusion that you do not believe what Christians believe. That's okay. You have the freedom to make your own choices, but at least you will have heard the Christian position and not rejected it in ignorance.

On the other hand, this book may help you come to believe that the Christian position is true. If that should happen, it would be good to find a church that teaches from the Bible so that you can grow and learn more about your new faith. Again, the choice is yours. The purpose of this book is also to present the Christian message to those believers who want to learn more about the faith they profess.

The Apostles' Creed[3]

The Apostles' Creed is a universally accepted *Statement of Faith* held by all Christian churches and denominations, as they feel it accurately summarizes the main teachings of the Bible. The basic text was found in many different forms as early as A.D. 150. The phrase *descended to the dead* is a late addition, appearing sometime after A.D. 600. In many Christian denominations, the Apostles' Creed is recited regularly on Sunday mornings. As a child growing up in the Lutheran Church, I remember memorizing this creed in confirmation class. It reads:

> I believe in God, the Father Almighty, Maker of heaven and earth. And in Jesus Christ, His only Son, our Lord; who was conceived by the Holy Spirit, born of the Virgin Mary; suffered under Pontius Pilate, was crucified, died and was buried. He descended to the dead. The third day He rose again from the dead; He ascended into heaven and sits on the right hand of God the

---

[3] The Apostles were the twelve men Jesus chose to be his main disciples who would pass on what they had learned from Jesus to others. The apostles did not write the Apostles' Creed, although the Creed is based on what they believed and taught.

Father Almighty; From there He shall come to judge the living and the dead.

I believe in the Holy Spirit, the Holy Christian Church, the Communion of Saints, the Forgiveness of sins, the Resurrection of the Body, and the Life Everlasting. Amen.

Since learning this creed in Confirmation class, and through studying such things as the Bible, history, and philosophy, and through my personal experiences, I have come to believe what is stated here is really true. My acceptance of these things has not just been on an intellectual level, but has profoundly affected the very way I live my life and relate to the world around me.

What do *you* believe? Let's journey together as I share with you some of the things I've discovered, so that you can also come to some conclusions about the Christian faith.

chapter one

I Believe

Before we eat food, it is good to wash our hands so that unwanted bacteria doesn't get in the way of our meal. In the same way, we need to clear away some common misconceptions about having a belief before we begin. In this chapter, we will look at a few of these belief fallacies:

a) It's all one—"Everything is equally true."
b) It's all relative—"Nothing can be known."
c) It's blind faith—"I believe in belief."

It's All One—
"Everything is Equally True"

To believe in everything is impossible. When we believe in everything, things lose their distinctiveness. It would make writing and reading words to convey an idea impossible, because we would have no standards or definitions on which to base their meaning.

If everything has equal validity, we have no basis for saying there is any difference between a great piece of art and child pornography, except for personal taste. If everything is the same, there are no categories by which to judge anything. If a tree, a rock, the wind, humanity, and divinity are all the same, we cannot give them separate titles.

If all things are the same, then everything—from food groups to animal kingdoms, to grammar to mathematics—becomes nonsensical, because by having them we are really saying things are different. If everything is true, all that exists is merely part of a big blob. The ability to communicate would be futile, because to do so uses certain words in a certain way, while not using others in another way.

The "all is true" philosophy may sound wonderful on the surface, but in reality, it leaves no room for individual personality, beauty, love, and discovery. "All is true" is not only impossible—it is a universal *blah*!

Many people can see that this "everything is equally true" way of thinking does not match everyday reality, and so they rightly reject it. Yet, when these same people approach religion, they feel that this basic logic no longer applies. Arguments such as, "Since there are so many religions, and Christianity [or whatever other faith] is a religion, Christianity [or whatever other faith] must be the same as all the others," are made. The problem is that this is too simplistic. It is the same as saying, "Since there are billions of guys in the world and Stefano Piva is a guy, every guy must be the same as Stefano Piva." I should hope not!

It is true that there are some aspects of being a guy that I have in common with all other guys, but that does not mean I am *identical* to every other guy. The same is true about religion, and some of the points of difference between the religions are major. Just from the surface, we know that some religions believe in only one God (Christians), others believe in many gods (Hindus), and others don't believe in a god at all (Buddhists). Obviously, these faiths cannot be equally true when they contradict each other from the very beginning. Again, the belief that "everything is true" is just too simplistic.

Things are not all the same. We need to make good or bad, true or false, and right or wrong distinctions.

It's All Relative—
"Nothing Can Be Known"

To say someone cannot believe in anything is just as impossible as saying that someone can believe in everything. Why? Because as soon as people say they don't believe in anything, they have just made a statement about what they *do* believe.

Claiming "I do not believe that anything can be known" is still a belief, even though it is stated in the negative. A belief in nothing falls into the exact same pitfall as a belief in everything. Saying we don't believe in something is to have an opinion about what we don't believe in. Even a belief in nothing is really a belief in something, and thus it also forces us into yes/no and either/or decisions. We cannot escape the law of non-contradiction.

It's Blind Faith—
"I Believe in Belief"

All this talk—about believing and not believing, and how we can know if what we believe is believable—is enough to give some people a brain freeze. A popular way out of this is to just believe whatever it is you believe in "by faith." I have talked to many Christians who consider this a pious answer in defense of their own faith, when in fact it is lazy and the very opposite of the kind of faith we find in the Bible. When the earliest Christian missionaries spoke, we read on a number of occasions that they attempted to *prove* their case,[4] and groups like the people of Berea *searched the Scriptures day after day to check up on Paul and Silas, to see if they*

---

[4] For example, Acts 9:22; 17:2–3,11,16; 18:4; 28; 26:19–25.

were really teaching the truth.[5] If you have ever met a Christian who told you to not ask questions and "just have faith," I want to apologize to you on that person's behalf.

Faith in faith is dangerous. Take the following example as an illustration. When we get on an airplane, we trust that the plane will stay in the air, and that the pilots know what they are doing. We put our faith in the reliability of the aircraft and its pilots, and trust that we will arrive at our destination safely. It would be foolish if we just hopped on any plane, even if it was half under construction or missing a wing, and say, "I believe by faith this plane will fly." We may even be really sincere about our belief— stupid, but sincere. The fact, however, is that a plane missing a wing cannot fly. There is no virtue in putting faith in our faith that the plane can fly.

In the same way, we don't just buy *any* house or car. We don't just put our money into *any* bank. We don't just marry *anyone*. We look into what we are doing, we check the facts, and then we put our faith in what appears to be worthy of our faith.

When it comes to religion, the same thing must be done. It is amazing that people will spend more time researching and deciding which colour to paint their house than on what or on whom they should stake their eternal destiny. Faith needs reasons. Having a belief just for the sake of it does not do anyone any good. It might make us feel good, but that doesn't mean that it is true. It could be a placebo belief. There is nothing special about belief. What is critical is the object of our belief.

How Can We Know What to Believe?

If we cannot believe in everything, and we cannot believe in nothing, and we can't escape thinking with the "just believe" approach, how do we know what to believe and whether it is true or not?

---

[5] Acts 17:11, NLT.

In the 1870s, a missionary by the name of Henry Stanley reached Uganda. When he arrived, he showed his Bible to King Mutesa of Uganda. After looking at the Bible, the chieftain told Stanley that the Muslims had also brought a book, the Koran, to him. "How do we know which is better?" Mutesa asked. "I am like a man in darkness. All I ask is that I be taught how to see."[6]

Today, faced with a number of different competing ideologies, many of us can relate to King Mutesa. But don't give up yet—keep reading!

One Other Barrier to Belief

As we begin wrestling with the claims of Christianity and whether they are believable or not, we need to mention one other possible obstacle that may hinder us from seeing clearly. Sometimes we say that we are openly seeking, but in reality, we don't really want to know the truth.

There will always be those who refuse to change their beliefs, even if they are shown to be wrong. Often this has nothing to do with evidence, but other issues. A famous preacher in the 1900s, Charles Spurgeon, gave an illustration of this. He shared a story of a man who was told that moons had been discovered around the planet Jupiter. The man refused to believe this new information, and so his friend brought him a telescope, set it up, and asked him to look and see for himself. The man still refused. "If I look and see that it does have moons," he said, "then I would have to believe that it does. Since I have no desire to believe this, I refuse to look in the telescope."[7]

The same can be true about religion. I have talked to many people who have rejected Christianity, but they have never looked

---

[6] Robert J. Morgan, *On This Day* (Nashville, TN: Thomas Nelson, 1997) Jan. 30.

[7] Charles Spurgeon, *Lectures to My Students* (Lynchburg, Virginia: The Old Time Gospel Hour, 1894) Book 3, p. 166.

into what Christians believe. There is not much we can do about this type of person, except to try and not to be like them.

What causes some people to resist changing their ideas even after they see the truth? It is the fact that a changed belief will affect the way a person lives. The Apostle Paul realized this, and that is why many of his letters in the New Testament follow the outline they do. Paul often started off by teaching doctrines and ideas about God, Christ, sin, salvation, the Holy Spirit, the Church, etc., and then ended by laying down ethical and lifestyle principles. Paul wrote his letters this way to teach that our beliefs have a direct impact on how we live. Paul's ethical principles followed his theology. For example, in Paul's letter to the Romans, after writing eleven chapters of theology he transitions into five chapters of ethics with the words: *And so, dear brothers and sisters, I plead with you to give your bodies to God. Let them be a living and holy sacrifice—the kind he will accept.*[8]

What we believe and how we live go hand in hand. This is a big reason why some people don't want to look through the telescope at Christianity—it is one thing to discover a new fact, but it is quite another when you realize this fact may call for a change of lifestyle.

Conclusion

Everyone believes. Everyone has faith. Everyone is religious. What we believe really does matter.

We have begun this study with a brief introduction to the Apostles' Creed, as well as a brief rebuttal of some of the roadblocks that may distort our vision. Let us now begin the journey through the Christian Creed.

---

[8] Rom. 12:1, NLT.

chapter two

I Believe in God, the Father Almighty, Maker of Heaven and Earth

As confidently as I can say, "I believe in God, the Father Almighty, Maker of heaven and earth," there are others who deny the very existence of God. In the late 1800s, Nietzsche proclaimed, "God is dead, we wander through an endless nothingness." The problem with Nietzsche's statement is that Nietzsche forgot to tell God that he no longer existed!

Reports of Mark Twain's death once flooded the United States. When Twain heard about this, he quickly sent out a cable, stating "The reports of my death are greatly exaggerated." Similarly, Nietzsche's reports of the death of God were also highly exaggerated.

Very few people disbelieve in the existence of God.[9] A survey done in 2000 found that eighty percent of Canadians claim to believe in God.[10] The creed "I believe in God" is not a stretch for

---

[9] Not that this matters. Whether people believe in God or not doesn't make him exist or not.

[10] Reginald Bibby, *Restless Gods* (Toronto, ON: Stoddart, 2002) p. 164.

most people. The *kind* of a god they believe in is another question.

Some people believe in God because they think they *are* God. Others follow a philosophy that says things like, "We are god, all is god, we are all part of a cosmic oneness." Hindus believe in millions of gods. Buddhists don't believe in any God. Muslims believe in one God. Christians believe in one Trinitarian God.

When we see these differences, and this is barely touching the surface, it is strange that seventy-two percent of Canadians agree with the statement, "All world religions are equally valid."[11] This may simply prove Canadians have very little knowledge regarding different world religions. It seems we want to believe in God, but are lost in knowing what to believe about God.

The Mystery

To presume to speak about God is a daunting task. If God does exist, how do we, who are minuscule compared with the size of the universe, talk about someone who is bigger than—as well as the Creator of—that universe? This planet we live on is only a speck of dust in the cosmos. It is impossible for us to wrap our minds around the size of the universe, with entire galaxies existing light-years away. How, then, can we begin to understand God?

Thomas Edison's line about our limited knowledge seems appropriate: "We do not know a millionth part of one percent of anything." Wouldn't such an all-powerful being or force be so beyond us that it would be impossible to comprehend? Is it even possible to talk about God?

In many ways God is incomprehensible, as the Bible very clearly demonstrates. In both Exodus and Deuteronomy, we have the story of God speaking to Moses on Mount Sinai, where he gave Moses the Ten Commandments. As the people of Israel realized what had happened, we read their response to Moses:

---

11 Donald Posterski, *True To You* (Winfield, BC: Wood Lake, 1995), p. 66.

The LORD our God has shown us his glory and greatness, and we have heard his voice from the heart of the fire. Today we have seen God speaking to humans, and yet we live! But now, why should we die? If the LORD our God speaks to us again, we will certainly die and be consumed by this awesome fire. Can any living thing hear the voice of the living God from the heart of the fire and yet survive? You go and listen to what the LORD our God says. Then come and tell us everything he tells you, and we will listen and obey.[12]

In trying to understand the vast size of God, the biblical Prophet Isaiah recorded these words:

This is what the LORD says: "Heaven is my throne, and the earth is my footstool. Could you ever build me a temple as good as that? Could you build a dwelling place for me? My hands have made both heaven and earth, and they are mine. I, the LORD, have spoken!"[13]

God is beyond comprehension!

I Believe in God

The first stanza of the Apostles' Creed reads, "I believe in God the Father Almighty, Maker of heaven and earth." How can Christians make this statement and presume to *know* anything about God, let alone that he exists as the Creator, the Almighty, and Father? Does this Christian belief in God have any validity to it? Is it simply wishful thinking, as individuals like Marx and Freud believed?

As has been already stated, Christians do recognize that God is beyond comprehension, but this is not the conclusion—it is simply *one* of the facts about God. The fact that God is incomprehensible doesn't mean that he is completely unknowable.

---

[12] Deut. 5:24–27, NLT.

[13] Isa. 66:1–2, NLT.

As Christians, we believe that we can know things about God because God has chosen to show himself to the world. Our talk about God has nothing to do with a superior knowledge or a great mystical insight, but stems from the fact that God has chosen to tangibly reveal his attributes to humanity in space and in history. In many ways, that is what the rest of this book is about—the tangible ways in which God has taken the effort to show himself to humanity so that we can know him. It is not about what we have discovered, but what God has revealed. One of the ways God has shown himself, stated in the first stanza of the Apostles' Creed, is through his creation.

Creator of Heaven and Earth

In Paul's letter to the Romans, he wrote:

From the time the world was created, people have seen the earth and sky and all that God made. They can clearly see his invisible qualities—his eternal power and divine nature. So they have no excuse whatsoever for not knowing God.[14]

For some people, science has pushed aside the need for God, but science doesn't answer any of life's basic questions:

1. What was first?
2. Where did the first thing(s) come from?
3. Where did nature get her laws?
4. How did life begin?
5. How has our brain come to know anything?
6. Where do morality and conscience come from?
7. Why does every civilization that ever existed worship something?

Science may try to come up with theories for these questions, but these step out of the realm of science and into the realm of

---

[14] Rom. 1:20, NLT.

philosophy and even theology. Science can merely explain observable facts, which only tell us what has happened in a particular situation at a specific time.

Therefore, to make a statement regarding our origins, using these facts, is to assume that the circumstances, environmental conditions, and specifics have always been the same, from the time of our origins until now. This, however, is not necessarily so. Much of what is presented as science, by organizations like *National Geographic,* is merely religious faith using scientific jargon. True science and God are not antagonists. A number of credible scientists and writers today have begun to challenge many of our society's so-called scientifically held assumptions.[15]

In the Jewish Scriptures, what Christians refer to as the Old Testament, we read: *The heavens tell of the glory of God. The skies display his marvelous craftsmanship. Day after day they continue to speak; night after night they make him known.*[16]

The Bible teaches us that God has shown himself to us through his creation in a way that should be obvious to all. Creation assumes a Creator. It actually takes less faith to believe this than to assume creation did not have a Creator and simply created itself.

The Almighty

The creation around us tells us more about God than the simple fact that there is a Creator. We also see that anyone who could put together something as large and complex as the universe, as well as something so small and complex as the human eyeball, must be the most powerful and intelligent being alive.

Again, we read in the Scriptures, this time from the Old Testament Prophet Jeremiah, *God made the earth by his power,*

---

[15] If you would like to delve into this more deeply, check out *Darwin's Black Box* by Michael Behe (Simon & Schuster; New York, NY, 1996), and *Darwin on Trial* by Philip Johnson (IVP; Downers Grove, IL, 1991).

[16] Ps. 19:1–2, NLT.

and he preserves it by his wisdom. He has stretched out the heavens by his understanding.[17]

In the New Testament, we read from Paul:

He made the things we can see and the things we can't see—kings, kingdoms, rulers, and authorities. Everything has been created through him and for him. He existed before everything else began, and he holds all creation together.[18]

According to the Bible, no one is mightier than God. He is the very definition of power. He is wisdom and understanding. These are not character traits he decided to have one day—they are who he is.

Since God created all things, with power, wisdom, and understanding, he was able to look at his creation and declare it very good.[19] At this point you may ask, "If God is the Creator of everything, and if he is all powerful, and if everything he created is very good, why are there things in the world like sickness, suffering, pain, and death?" That is a good question.

The Problem

As I stated earlier in this chapter, there is a danger in assuming that the way things are now is the way things have always been. According to the Bible, there was a time when sin and evil did not exist. God, in his mercy and love for us, gave us the free choice to either choose to go God's way or our own way, and humanity chose their own way.

By allowing this choice, God opened up the possibility for evil—which is choosing against the one whose very character is goodness. Evil is not another creation, but anti-creation. Sin takes God's good creation and twists it in a way that is against his will. What was meant to bring life ends up bringing death. The creation

---

[17] Jer. 10:12, NLT.

[18] Col. 1:16–17, NLT.

[19] Gen. 1:31.

and humanity we see today is scarred, but even the ability to recognize this points to a standard of goodness.

Another question that may be asked is, "Why did God allow this possibility to exist in his creation?" Ultimately, we do not know the answer to that question. Knowing that God is a God of love, we must assume that God's allowing us to have the choice to love him, at the risk of sin, was of higher importance to him then a sinless universe with human beings made to love him (which isn't love at all).[20]

God Almighty, Creator of heaven and earth, is the same God who desires a relationship with humanity to such an extent that he gave (and still gives) us the free choice to choose for or against him. We see from this that God is not only an all-powerful Creator, but personal.

God the Father

As a personal God, another way in which God has chosen to reveal himself is as a Father. God is not simply a force, but a person. Some people today get bent out of shape by hearing God referred to as a father. There are a couple of reasons for this—first, some people have had a negative example of a father in their earthly father. Second, some people feel that the idea of God as a father simply comes from a patriarchal culture, which needs updating for our times. Let's deal with each of these in turn.

For those whose earthly fathers were a bad example, we need to realize God is *not* a reflection of our earthly father. That is getting the tail and the head mixed up. God is the standard of fatherhood, and the Bible teaches that God is a loving, kind, forgiving, merciful, just, longsuffering, and patient Father. In fact, every earthly father falls short of the true fatherhood of God. God is the perfection of fatherhood, which some earthly fathers have failed miserably at modeling, while others strive to this good example.

---

[20] We will talk more about this whole issue of sin and what God has done about it in chapter four.

Let us now look at the point about the fatherhood of God merely being a patriarchal cultural projection. It is correct to say that God is not actually male in the sense of having male genitalia, as was often depicted with pagan idols. God is *more* than male. God is all the perfect attributes of personhood, both male and female, and in some ways we could even say he is transpersonal. However, God has chosen to reveal himself to us as a Father. This is confirmed in that Jesus continually referred to God as his Father, and never as his mother. We know that God is more, but should refer to him as Christ taught us—"Our Father."[21]

An interesting point to consider, for those who believe they need to "update" God with "Mother/Father" or even gender-neutral terms—the monotheistic fatherhood of God we find in the Bible was not cultural, but counter-cultural, for its day. The neighbouring nations were all known for their goddesses.

Israel's danger lay in trying to make the God revealed to them fit in better with the surrounding nations. A monotheistic Father God was not something that came out of Israel's culture. In fact, it was often an embarrassing uniqueness for them. God's revealing himself as a Father was God's doing despite Israel, not because of Israel. In the same way, as Christians, we share what we believe God has revealed, not what we would like God to say about himself.

The first statement in the Apostles' Creed reads, "I believe in God the Father Almighty, Maker of heaven and earth." From this, we have seen that Christians believe:

1. God has revealed his existence.
2. God has revealed himself as the Creator.
3. God has revealed himself as the Almighty.
4. God has revealed himself as a personal Father.

---

21 Matt. 6:9.

Worship

We will never come close to fully understanding God, but that does not mean we cannot know anything about him. God has revealed himself to us so that we can know him and have a loving relationship with him. God is both knowable and incomprehensible, just as he is personal and transpersonal. It is good for us to remember this. We see both of these truths depicted in Isaiah's words, when he encountered the living God:

> *"My destruction is sealed, for I am a sinful man and a member of a sinful race. Yet I have seen the King, the LORD Almighty."*[22]
> *Then one of the seraphim flew over to the altar, and he picked up a burning coal with a pair of tongs. He touched my lips with it and said, "See, this coal has touched your lips. Now your guilt is removed, and your sins are forgiven."*
> *Then I heard the Lord asking, "Whom should I send as a messenger to my people? Who will go for us?"*
> *And I said, "Lord, I'll go! Send me."*
> *And he said, "Yes, go"* [and tell this people].[23]

We can talk about God, not because of anything special in us or because of our superior knowledge, but because God shown himself to humanity. As we are going to see in these upcoming chapters, God entered human history so that we could know him, be forgiven by him, and have an ongoing relationship with him. God can give us a new spirit and empower us to really live.

We have not discovered God; God has revealed himself to us. I cannot say, "I believe in God the Father Almighty, Creator of heaven and earth," because I found him, but because *he*

---

[22] Isa. 6:5, NLT.

[23] Isa. 6:7–9, NLT.

found *me*. The knowledge of these things fills us with awe and leads us right back into the mystery of God.

> *Fear of the* LORD *is the beginning of wisdom. Knowledge of the Holy One results in understanding.*[24]

---

chapter three

I Believe in Jesus Christ, His Only Son Our Lord, Conceived by the Holy Spirit, Born of the Virgin Mary

Jesus Christ has been more admired and more misunderstood than any other person in history. He has been labeled an imposter, a heretic, a good teacher, a victim, an idealist, a prophet, and God in the flesh!

When Jesus walked this earth, he talked about love and judgment. He played with children and hung around with prostitutes and tax collectors. He called many of the religious teachers hypocrites, snakes, whitewashed tombs, and a brood of vipers on their way to hell.

Jesus believed in a literal devil and talked with evil spirits. Jesus healed people, physically, spiritually, and emotionally. He never married, he had no home, he was executed by Roman crucifixion in his thirties, and his followers claimed that he rose from the dead.

During his life on earth, Jesus had many encounters with different individuals. One time, a rich man who would have been happy to tithe well over ten percent told Jesus that he wanted to be one of his followers. Jesus asked him to give up everything he owned.[25] On another occasion, a crowd wanted to make Jesus their king, until Jesus said they had to eat his flesh and drink his blood.[26] There was also the time a religious teacher asked Jesus to show him the Kingdom of God, and Jesus told him the only way he could do this was if he went through the birth process a second time.[27] When we read through the gospels,[28] we find these are only a few of the many "strange encounters" people had with Jesus.

In the first two chapters of this book, we talked about beliefs and about God. Now we face the question, "Who is Jesus?" This is a huge question, because it is at the very heart of Christianity. In fact, the very name *Christian* finds its origins in Jesus' followers,[29] causing some theologians to state, "Christianity is Christ." The answer to the question, "Who is Jesus?" is the foundation of Christianity.

Who is Jesus?

This question is not simply a unique question for today's inquiring minds. The question has been asked ever since Jesus set foot on the earth.

In Matthew's Gospel, we read, *When Jesus came to the region of Caesarea Philippi, he asked his disciples, "Who do people say the Son of Man is?"*[30] The term "Son of man" was a title Jesus used often when referring to himself. In this instance, Jesus asked his disciples, "Who are people saying I am?" Today, Jesus would be asking, "When you listen to the talk shows and see the latest movies, or read the newest books about me, who are people saying I am?"

---

25 Matt. 19:16–30.

26 John 6.

27 John 3.

28 Matthew, Mark, Luke, and John.

29 Acts 11:26.

30 Matt. 16:13, NLT.

The account in Matthew goes on; *"Well,"* they replied, *"some say John the Baptist, some say Elijah, and others say Jeremiah or one of the other prophets."* [31] Today, some people see Jesus as a moral teacher, others see him as a founder of a religion, some simply know his name as a swear, others see him as a prophet, and still others see a man who got in touch with his inner divinity.

Then he (Jesus) *asked them, "Who do you say that I am?"* [32]

Jesus looked his disciples in the eyes and said, "Okay, that's what people are saying about me, but who do *you* say I am?" Today, Jesus is asking each of us this question as well. *Simon Peter answered, "You are the Messiah, the Son of the living God."* [33]

Peter's profession of faith and his acknowledgement and acceptance of Jesus as the Christ changed his life forever. Peter believed Jesus to be the Lord and Christ promised in the Old Testament Scriptures, and it was upon this confession that Jesus told Peter he would build his church. [34] It is little wonder, then, that the title, "the Lord Jesus Christ," or "Jesus Christ our Lord," became the earliest confession of the church. [35] A phrase picked up in the Apostles' Creed: "I believe in *Jesus Christ*, his only Son *our Lord*; who was conceived by the Holy Spirit, born of the Virgin Mary."

If the Church was founded on the belief that Jesus was Christ and Lord, it is important for us to understand what the Church meant by these terms. Who did the early followers of Jesus believe he was?

In the first stanza about Christ in the Apostles' Creed, the writers answered the question "Who is Jesus?" with four doctrinal statements.

---

[31] Matt. 16:14, NLT.

[32] Matt. 16:15, NLT.

[33] Matt. 16:16, NLT.

[34] Matt. 16:15–20.

[35] See Gal. 1:3, 1 and 2 Thess. 1:1–2 (three of the earliest Christian writings—A.D. 49–52).

They went on to say more about Christ, but for the remainder of this chapter, we will look at these four statements. They are:

1. Jesus is the Christ.
2. Jesus is the Son of God.
3. Jesus is Lord.
4. Jesus' origins are not natural, but supernatural.

Jesus is the Christ

The word "Christ" was not Jesus' last name. It was a title given to him. When the Bible refers to Jesus as "Jesus Christ" or "Christ Jesus," it is using Christ in the same way that some people refer to me as *Pastor* Stefano, or Stefano *our Pastor*, or the way you may refer to your *doctor* as *Doctor* Whoever. The title implies the individual's role and a description of what they do. In the same way, the title "Christ" refers to Jesus' role and a description of what he came to do.

The first Christians recognized Jesus as the Old Testament-promised Messiah, who was to come and save his people. The Hebrew word *Messiah* meant "anointed," or "anointed one," and its Greek equivalent was *Christ*. The early church was founded on Peter's confession that Jesus was the *Messiah* (in Hebrew), the *Christ* (in Greek), sent to us by God to save us from our sins (our choosing against God).

Jesus is the Son of God

The term "Son of God" has often been misunderstood. "Son of God," like "Christ," is a title, a role, and a description of the relationship Jesus has with his Heavenly Father—it is neither a biological reality nor does it indicate a chronological order to the divinity.[36] The Bible teaches us that Jesus co-existed eternally with

---

36 John 1:1–4 and 14, Col. 1:15–20, Heb. 1:1–4. Also, Jesus is called the "Lamb of God,"—this does not mean that he is a literal lamb with wool, but that he plays the role of a lamb through his sacrificial death. "Son of God," like "Lamb of God" is a descriptive title for Jesus' role.

the Father. Speaking about Jesus, Paul writes, *he existed before everything else began, and he holds all creation together.*[37]

In regards to the title "Son of God," some people ask, "How is this unique to Jesus? Are not all God's children sons and daughters of God?" The answer to that is yes and no—the Bible refers to Christians as sons and daughters of God *by adoption,*[38] but Jesus is God's Son in the fact that he shares *the same nature* as his Father. That is how this phrase is unique to Jesus.

Jesus' contemporaries recognized that Jesus was claiming to be more than a creation and follower of his Heavenly Father. When Jesus made the statement, *"The Father and I are one,"* we read that,

Once again the Jewish leaders picked up stones to kill him. Jesus said, "At my Father's direction I have done many things to help the people. For which one of these good deeds are you killing me?" They replied, "Not for any good work, but for blasphemy, because you, a mere man, have made yourself God."[39]

As we are going to see at a few points in this study, we run into a mystery that Christians throughout the ages have referred to as the Trinity. "The Trinity" is a term used to describe what the Bible teaches about God: that there is only one God, but the full attributes of divinity are held by God the Father, Jesus Christ, and the Holy Spirit.

In order to define this paradox, Christians have taught that there is one God, but he exists as three persons. God is one community of three individuals in perfect harmony and love with one another. Morality finds its origins in the character of this God who has eternally existed in relationship. Ultimately we will never fully understand this aspect of God, and Christians have run into danger by trying to define it too precisely. As we said in our last chapter,

---

[37] Col. 1:17, NLT (see also John 1:1–5 and 14).

[38] Rom. 8:12–17 and 23, Gal. 4:1–7, Eph. 1:4–6.

[39] John 10:30–33, NLT.

many things about God are beyond our comprehension. That's why he is God![40]

The Apostles' Creed and the Bible refer to Jesus as the "Son of God," as a description of his unique connection with divinity and to describe the relationship Jesus has with his Heavenly Father.

It is not enough for a Christian to acknowledge these facts. Yes, Jesus is the Christ and, therefore, the Saviour and Messiah. Yes, Jesus is the Son of God and, therefore, divine, and one with God the Father in a unique relational way. But a Christian confession is also; "I believe in Jesus Christ, his only Son *our Lord.*"

Jesus is Lord

What did the New Testament writers mean when they called Jesus "Lord"? The word often used for "Lord" in the Old Testament, when referring to God, was the Hebrew word *Adonai*. The Greek word for *Adonai* was *Kurios*, and this exact word is used to refer to Jesus as "Lord" in the New Testament. This is profound, and again we are faced with the paradox of the Trinity.

Paul uses the term "Lord" for Jesus 222 times—and in many of these instances, he uses *Kurios*. When Paul refers to Jesus as "Lord" (*Kurios/Adonai*), he clearly sees him as the same God revealed in the Old Testament. They are both *Adonai*! Paul writes, *If you confess with your mouth, "Jesus is Lord," and believe in your heart that God raised him from the dead, you will be saved.*[41]

To confess that Jesus is Lord means to recognize him as *our* Messiah and Christ, under whose divinity we operate, and that we have chosen to submit ourselves to him. God is God, whether we believe in him or not. He is the Ruler, whether we submit to him or not. If Jesus is really who he said he was, then he is the Lord over all, no matter what.

---

[40] See the beginning of chapter seven for a further discussion on the Trinity.

[41] Rom. 10:9, NLT.

To be a Christian, however, means willfully accepting Jesus as *our* Lord. It is personally surrendering our life to his will, and choosing to follow him. The writers of the Apostles' Creed were not simply stating facts they had discovered; they were confessing that they had personally accepted Jesus as their Lord (*Kurios/Adonai*).

To do this is to say, "Jesus, you can have control of my life, my family, my possessions." It is to say, "I surrender all," like when Peter said to Jesus, *"We have given up everything to follow you."* [42] This is exactly where Jesus' self-recognition of his lordship goes beyond his simply being a good teacher. Dick France, the principal of Wycliffe Hall Theological College in Oxford, England, wrote:

> He called people to believe in him, to trust him, to be loyal to him before all other loyalties. He invited them to come to him, and he would give them rest. He declared that in the final judgment they would be judged by their response to him, indeed that he himself would be the judge, pronouncing final sentences on all nations on the basis of the way they had treated him. He claimed that he could give life, because he had life in himself. He spoke not only of God's kingdom, but of his own kingdom. He said that to reject or to receive him was to reject or receive God. [43]

When we read about Jesus, we find a person who saw himself as Lord, as equal with God, as the one who holds our destiny in his hands, and the one to whom we must bow the knee. We have to conclude that he is either Lord or the most arrogant man who ever lived—there is no middle ground.

Jesus Supernaturally Conceived

One further confession about Jesus, from this stanza of the creed, states; "I believe in Jesus Christ, his only Son our Lord; who was conceived by the Holy Spirit, born of the Virgin Mary."

---

[42] Matt. 19:27, NLT.

[43] Dick France, *Exploring The Christian Faith* (Nashville. TN: Thomas Nelson, 1996) p. 73.

In Matthew's Gospel, we read that Mary *became pregnant by the Holy Spirit.*[44] Luke records in his Gospel that when the angel announced Mary would have a child she answered, *"But how can I have a baby? I am a virgin."*

> *The angel replied, "The Holy Spirit will come upon you, and the power of the Most High will overshadow you. So the baby born to you will be holy, and he will be called the Son of God. What's more, your relative Elizabeth has become pregnant in her old age! People used to say she was barren, but she's already in her sixth month. For nothing is impossible with God."*[45]

Since we have already addressed Jesus' co-existence with his Heavenly Father, we can affirm Jesus did not come into existence at his earthly conception. We are speaking of divine things, and we must affirm what has been revealed to us and be careful not to try and explain how God did it.

What the Bible and the Apostles' Creed both affirm is that Jesus always existed. Mary never slept with any man before she gave birth to Jesus. Through a miracle of the Holy Spirit, Jesus became human and implanted himself in Mary's womb. Jesus was delivered as a real human baby and lived a life as a real human being, yet without sin.[46] The unique events surrounding Jesus' birth were further proof to Jesus' followers that this individual was more than just a man.

Summary

Jesus' followers recognized him as the promised Christ who had come as their Saviour and Messiah. They recognized him as the Son of God, making him a divine being. They recognized that Jesus was in a unique eternal relationship with God the Father and the

---

44 Matt. 1:18, NLT.

45 Luke 1:34–37, NLT.

46 Heb. 4:15.

Holy Spirit. Jesus' followers recognized him as the Lord of all, to whom they personally owed their allegiance. They also recognized, by the unique events surrounding Jesus' physical birth, that there was something supernatural about this person from Nazareth.

Jesus' disciple John was convinced of these things, and fully gave his life over to him. In some of the closing remarks in his Gospel, he wrote, *These are written so that you may believe that Jesus is the Messiah, the Son of God, and that by believing in him you will have life.*[47] That is a very similar claim to the statement in the Apostles' Creed: "We believe in Jesus Christ his only Son our Lord; who was conceived by the Holy Spirit, born of the Virgin Mary."

Conclusion—It's About Relationship

One of the greatest ways we have misunderstood Jesus today is by trying to tone him down and tame him. We do this because Jesus is much more easy to deal with if we can comfortably fit him into our lifestyle, but Jesus is not going to fit into anyone's formula.

Christianity is not about mastering a ritual to appease Jesus. Instead, it is about developing a personal relationship with him—and relationships are dangerous. Even earthly relationships are risky. This makes it popular and safe to be constantly not ready "to make a commitment."

We like formulas, rituals, and religion, because they are measurable and put us in control. They teach us that, as long as we do certain things in such a way so many times, we are okay. The thing is, the only way to know Jesus is through a relationship with him, and a relationship with Jesus is not going to be comfortable.

Jesus is always on the move, always changing things, always challenging the status quo, always pushing our buttons, always probing deeper. As soon as we think we've got him figured out or think we have arrived, Jesus shows we've just begun. Jesus wants to build our character. He asks us to do crazy things that don't seem

---

[47] John 20:31, NLT.

to make sense at the time. He wants us to stick our necks on the line and grow deeper as people. He sends interruptions and inconveniences because it is in these that we often meet him. Jesus asks us to walk by faith, not sight. Ultimately, Jesus wants us to love him and love those around us. Jesus isn't calling us to a religion, but to a relationship.

Who do you see when you look at Jesus? How are you going to answer Jesus' question, "Who do *you* say that I am?"

chapter four

I Believe That Jesus Suffered Under Pontius Pilate, was Crucified, Died, and Buried, and Descended to the Dead

There is a group of Hmong people in the United States who escaped from Laos' political and military corruption. Back when they made their escape, they had to cross a shallow river, in which there was a mined bank. When they reached the bank in the middle of the night, the group couldn't tell where they were and were afraid to cross.

As they all stood wondering what to do, an old tribesman came forward and said, "I'm an old man; I'll go first." The man then walked slowly across the bank, putting one foot before the other, never knowing where his next step would land. Eventually, one step detonated a mine and he was killed instantly. By following this old man's path, the rest of the group was now able to get across. Today they are leading a church in Milwaukee, Wisconsin. This group exists because of one man's substitutionary death.

The stanza of the creed that is our focus for this chapter has some very painful words in it. We read that Jesus *suffered*, was *crucified*, *died*, was *buried,* and *descended.* A question must be asked—why do we have so many depressing and defeatist words connected to a person who, as we saw in the last chapter, many people worship as Lord?

In chapter two, we briefly mentioned the reality of sin in God's good creation. With sin, we have suffering, pain, death, decay, addiction, loneliness, and brokenness in every part of life. When Jesus came to this earth, he came to deal with the sin that distorted his creation. The surprise, however, is that Jesus chose to embrace the results of sin in order to turn things around. Through pain and death he brought healing and life. Paul understood this and that is why he wrote,

> *Now, no one is likely to die for a good person, though someone might be willing to die for a person who is especially good... yet, when we were utterly helpless, Christ came at just the right time and died for us sinners.*[48]

Jesus used *death* to do something for *helpless sinners.* Jesus came into this world as a real human, and never remained aloof or stoic from the pain of a fallen world. Jesus would never have agreed with the approach of a Buddhist monk who tries to find life by escaping suffering through self-denial. Instead, Jesus found and gave life through embracing suffering. Again, Paul wrote:

> *Your attitude should be the same that Christ Jesus had. Though he was God, he did not demand and cling to his rights as God. He made himself nothing; he took the humble position of a slave and appeared in human form. And in human form he obediently humbled himself even further by dying a criminal's death on a cross.*[49]

As has already been stated in this book, Jesus' ministry confused many people. Peter, one of his closest disciples, recognized

---

[48] Rom. 5:7 and 6, NLT.

[49] Phil. 2:5–8, NLT.

Jesus as the Christ/Messiah. The kind of Messiah Peter had been expecting, however, did not seem to be the one portrayed in the path Jesus was walking. Either Jesus wasn't the right Messiah, or Peter did not have the correct idea of who the Messiah was going to be.

In Peter's day, the Jews were looking for a warlord Messiah, who would raise an army, set up his kingdom, and defeat the Romans. When the disciples lived through the historical event of Jesus' trial and death, they abandoned him, denied him, and hid, for they thought their Messiah was defeated. Jesus, however, came on a mission in which suffering and dying would play a major part. Only later did many of Jesus' followers understand—many, however, still did not. That problem still exists today. Let's look at this stanza of the creed and see if we can better understand why Jesus' life and ministry included suffering, crucifixion, and death.

Jesus *Suffered* under Pontius Pilate

Jesus' suffering under Pontius Pilate is the ultimate irony of history. Here we have the Creator of all things *suffering* under an unstable political ruler. It is an interesting fact that the writers of the creed included the name of a relatively insignificant Roman ruler, but they did so for a specific reason. In Jesus' day, they did not have a calendar to date events like we have today—significant events or people were recorded in history based on the dates and reign of kings. We see this throughout the Old Testament.[50] By placing the name Pontius Pilate into the creed, the writers were being careful to record what was *historical.* It was something that happened on this earth, in a real place, and under the time of a real ruler.

Pontius Pilate was an appointed Roman governor from A.D. 26–36 in the region of Palestine. The Roman historian Tacitus, who lived between A.D. 55 and 117, confirms this in his *Annals* with the words, "Christ, who got his name from a group the populace called

---

[50] For example, "In the year that King Uzziah died," (Is. 6:1).

Christians... suffered the extreme penalty during the reign of Tiberius at the hands of one of our procurators, Pontius Pilate."[51]

The Pilate we see in the pages of the Bible comes across as a fairly weak character. When the priests brought Jesus before him with the charge that he was calling himself a king, Pilate saw right through their ploy; but because of the pressure of the populace, Pilate condemned Jesus anyway. Knowing that Jesus was an innocent man, and to try and relieve his guilt, Pilate washed his hands in a bowl of water and publicly declared himself innocent of Jesus' blood.

If Jesus was who he said he was, he could have destroyed Pilate by calling down an army of angels to crush him. Jesus never did, because of a greater plan he had—which at that point no one but Jesus understood. Pilate may have thought *he* was in control, but Jesus *knew* that he was in total control.

When Pilate questioned Jesus about his identity and Jesus stood by quietly, Pilate said, "*You won't talk to me... Don't you realize that I have the power to release you or to crucify you?*"

Jesus simply looked at Pilate and said, "*You would have no power over me at all unless it were given to you from above.*"[52]

On another occasion, as Pilate was investigating the charges brought against Jesus, he asked him, "Are you a king?"

Jesus answered, "*I am not an earthly king. If I were, my followers would have fought when I was arrested by the Jewish leaders. But my kingdom is not of this world.*"[53]

If you were Pilate, what would be going though your head if you heard someone respond to your questions this way?

The Apostles' Creed tells us Jesus willingly *suffered under Pontius Pilate*. How did this suffering look? According to the Gospel accounts, Jesus was spit upon, had his beard ripped out, was mocked and punched in the face. The Roman soldiers whipped

---

51 Tacitus, *Annals,* XV, #44.

52 John 19:10–11, NLT.

53 John 18:36, NLT.

Jesus' back, jammed a crown of thorns onto his head, and beat him with a stick. They made him carry his own cross to his execution site, where he would be nailed up for all to see, and left to die.

Why would Jesus go through this? What did Jesus understand that allowed him to go through such pain and humiliation?

Jesus Was Crucified

Jesus allowed himself to be nailed to a cross and suffer crucifixion. Again, if he was who he said he was, he could have saved himself.[54] Instead he took on embarrassment, emptiness, and filth.

To be hung up on a cross was one of the most shameful ways to die. Even in the Old Testament, before cross crucifixion was practiced, we read; *Anyone hanging on a tree is cursed of God.*[55] Jesus had nails rammed through his feet and wrists, as well as his body tied to wooden planks. Even though in most crucifix pictures Jesus is wearing a cloth around his waist, the reality is that he probably would have been hung totally naked. His bloody body would have attracted flies and birds, and his nailed arms would not have been able to push them away.

Jesus would have had to continually push himself up on his nail-pierced feet in order to breathe. Most criminals died of suffocation long before they bled to death, for they needed to continually straighten themselves up in order to breathe. This is why the Roman soldiers would sometimes break the legs of criminals—it quickened their death.

It was also a common practice to have the criminal's name and crime written above their head, so that everybody passing by would know why the person was there. It would also serve as a warning against committing the same crime. For Jesus, the sign above his head read, "Jesus, King of the Jews."

Crucifixion was such a torturous method of death that even Herod the Great, who was involved in all kinds of horrific acts, like

---

[54] Luke 23:39.

[55] Deut. 21:23, NLT.

killing his own family members and massacring little children,[56] refused to allow the distasteful crucifixion to be used on his enemies.

Everything I've described so far is only the physical pain Jesus went through. Even greater pain would have been the inner emotional suffering Jesus experienced as everyone deserted him, unable to understand him. Jesus' greatest pain, however, was the spiritual abandonment he endured as his Father turned away from his Son when Jesus took upon himself the sins of the world. From the cross, Jesus cried out; *"My God, my God, why have you forsaken me?"* [57]

Jesus was crucified. He chose this. The question we cannot help but ask is *why*? Why would anyone choose this?

Died, Buried, Descended

When they came to Jesus, they saw that he was dead already, so they didn't break his legs. One of the soldiers, however, pierced his side with a spear, and blood and water flowed out. [58]

Jesus really died—his mind stopped, his breath ceased. He was no more. When they took his lifeless body off the cross, a man named Joseph from Arimathea asked Pilate for Jesus' body so that he could bury it. We read in the Bible that Joseph was a disciple of Jesus' who was a wealthy man, and he provided Jesus' body with a new tomb in a garden.[59,60]

---

[56] Matt. 2.

[57] Matt. 27:46, NLT.

[58] John 19:33–34, NLT.

[59] Matt. 27:57–58, Mark 15:42–43, Luke 23:50–52.

[60] What happened to Jesus when he died? There have been many speculations. The Bible, however, is unclear. What we know for sure is that Jesus, himself, really died for three days. It was not just his physical body that died. See the last chapter for more clarification on what happens to us when we die.

What is the Point of All This Suffering?

Jesus suffered, was crucified, dead, buried, and descended to the dead. None of these things happened to him out of his control. It was part of his plan to embrace the pain of this sinful world in order to save it. Jesus came into this world knowing full well what his mission was. Seven hundred years before he came to this earth, the prophet Isaiah wrote:

> *He was despised and rejected—a man of sorrows, acquainted with bitterest grief. We turned our backs on him and looked the other way when he went by. He was despised and we did not care.*
>
> *Yet it was our weakness he carried; it was our sorrows that weighed him down. And we thought his troubles were a punishment from God for his own sins! But he was wounded and crushed for our sins. He was beaten that we might have peace. He was whipped, and we were healed! All of us have strayed away like sheep. We have left God's path to follow our own. Yet the Lord laid on him the guilt and sins of us all.*
>
> *He was oppressed and treated harshly, yet he never said a word. He was led as a lamb to the slaughter. And as a sheep is silent before the shearers, he did not open his mouth. From prison and trial they led him away to his death. But who among the people realized that he was dying for their sins— that he was suffering their punishment? He had done no wrong, and he never deceived anyone. But he was buried like a criminal; he was put in a rich man's grave.*[61]

So here we have it! Jesus willingly went through all of this because he had each of us in mind. He suffered to relieve suffering people, he put himself in bondage to free people in bondage, and he became sin in order to forgive sinful people. Jesus embraced the

---

[61] Is. 53:3–9, NLT.

shame, the death, and the burial we deserved. It should have been our crucifixion, for the penalty for sin is death.[62]

But who among the people realized that he was dying for their sins—that he was suffering their punishment? Jesus took our place on the cross. He allowed the Father to forsake him so that he would not have to forsake us. Our sinful past can now be buried. Jesus, like that Hmong tribesman, went before us. He provided our path to freedom. Paul wrote:

> *For all have sinned; all fall short of God's glorious standard. Yet now God in his gracious kindness declares us not guilty. He has done this through Christ Jesus, who has freed us by taking away our sins.*[63]

It is quite amazing when you think about it. Jesus knew that we were broken and hurting, and that we could not help ourselves. He knew that we needed a new life and a new start. He knew the only way that was going to happen was through death. So Jesus took it upon himself to face death. Jesus came to this world to die, because he was motivated by a love for his lost creation.

Jesus was not a helpless victim when he hung on the cross, but the victorious Messiah! If Jesus was who he said he was, it took more strength for him to remain on the cross than to come down off it. He had us in mind, and that caused him to persevere unto death. It has been said, "It was not nails that held Jesus to the cross, but love." That is why he suffered, was crucified, died, and was buried!

---

[62] Rom. 6:23.

[63] Rom. 3:23–24, NLT.

chapter five

I Believe That On the Third Day Jesus Rose From the Dead

Christians celebrate Easter because they believe Jesus "rose from the dead" three days after he "suffered, was crucified, and buried." This is an astonishing claim. Are we sure it is not wishful thinking?

Some people believe Easter involves chocolate eggs and a bunny. Should we put the story of Jesus' coming back to life again in the same category as the Easter Bunny? Are there any *reasons* we should believe the resurrection as fact? Let's face it, if it never happened, Christians are deceiving themselves, and I would hope that they would have the intellectual integrity to walk away from it.

We don't believe something because it is a nice story; we believe something because it is true. The Apostle Paul understood this when he wrote,

> *If Christ was not raised, then all our preaching is useless, and your trust in God is useless. And we apostles would all*

be lying about God, for we have said that God raised Christ from the grave.[64]

Paul saw the Church and her message as meaningless, if, after Christ's death, he did not really come back to life. In fact, Paul goes on to say that the Church's message is dangerous, if Christ has not been raised from the dead. The Church is then lying to people and filling minds with false hope.

If you read 1 Corinthians 15, to the end of verse 19, Paul says that if Christ has not been raised from the dead, our faith is futile, we are still lost to our sins, our loved ones who have passed away in the Lord are gone forever, and we who choose to follow Christ are really the most miserable people in the world. In fact, if there is no resurrection, *let's feast and get drunk, for tomorrow we die!*[65]

We can tell by these words that Paul felt a real resurrection was a non-negotiable fact for the Christian faith. On what basis did Paul believe in the resurrection of Christ? What were the *reasons* for his *faith*? Why was he willing to lay down his life for this truth?

The Church was also founded on the belief that Jesus Christ rose from the dead. Throughout church history, many individuals have been willing to lay down their lives for the truth of Jesus' resurrection. Did all these people die for a fairy tale? In this chapter, we are going to look at *why* the Church believes the statement in the Apostles' Creed, which states, "I believe that on the third day Jesus rose from the dead."

A little more than twenty years after the death of Jesus, the Apostle Paul wrote his first letter to the church in Corinth—around A.D. 55. In chapter fifteen of this letter, Paul passionately defends the resurrection of Christ. He sees it as the foundation upon which the Church stands or falls.[66] Beginning at verse three,

---

[64] 1 Cor. 15:14–15, NLT.

[65] 1 Cor. 15:32, NLT.

[66] I would encourage you to stop and read 1 Corinthians 15 right now.

let's walk through this chapter and pick up on five of the reasons Paul believed in the resurrection of Christ. In turn, we will see five reasons why we also can believe that Jesus rose from the dead.[67]

The First Reason Paul Believed Jesus Rose from the Dead

Paul writes, "*I passed on to you what was most important and what had also been passed on to me.*"[68] The first reason Paul believed in the resurrection of Christ was that:

It was not something that he made up, but something he *received*.

Some scholars try and claim Paul as the inventor of Christianity. They believe that Jesus was simply a good teacher whom Paul created into a divine being. The reality, from Paul's own words, is that he did not invent the story, or package a new system of religious thinking. Paul claimed to be speaking the truth as he received it.

---

[67] There are literally dozens of books that deal with the reasons one can believe in the resurrection. I would encourage you to read some of the following:

John N. Akers, John H. Armstrong, & John D. Woodbridge (Editors), *This We Believe*, Thomas Oden, "Did Jesus Really Rise from the Dead?" (Grand Rapids, MI: Zondervan, 2000), pp. 101–118.

Michael Green, *World on the Run*, (Leicester, England: InterVarsity, 1983) pp. 51–59.

George Eldon Ladd, *A Theology of the New Testament*, (Grand Rapids, MI: Eerdmans, 1974) pp. 315–327.

Josh McDowell, *Evidence That Demands a Verdict*, (San Bernardino, CA: Nelson, 1972) pp. 179–260.

Everett F. Harrison, *A Short Life of Christ*, (Grand Rapids, MI: Eerdmans, 1968) pp. 231–246.

[68] 1 Cor. 15:3, NLT.

A few years ago, an article written about the famous English author and Christian apologist C.S. Lewis went on to criticize Lewis for not being an original thinker. The writer said that Lewis never came up with any new ideas, but simply repackaged and rehashed old ones. Shortly after this article came out, another writer, commenting on the article about C.S. Lewis, wrote that Lewis would have taken it as a great compliment to be told that he was *not* original. This commentator continued by stating that C.S. Lewis never set out to be an original thinker; in fact, he was suspicious of many "new" ideas. For instance, Lewis believed that truth was to be found in the historical reality of Christ and in his resurrection; therefore, he set out to communicate something timeless, not something trendy.

Paul, like C.S. Lewis, was not teaching a new idea or philosophy he dreamt up. He did not try and start a new religion. This would have gone against his character. Before his conversion, Paul was a strict advocate of Orthodox Judaism. He was so convinced of this religious ideology that we find Paul, in Acts 7–8, on a mission to destroy the Church.[69] Something dramatic must have taken place to turn this persecutor of the Church into one of its most vocal spokesmen. In Acts 9, we find that it was Paul's encounter with the living, resurrected Christ that made the change. Paul's life was turned around by the fact that "on the third day Christ rose from the dead." This was not a story Paul made up, but a reality he encountered.

The Second Reason Paul Believed Jesus Rose from the Dead

Christ died for our sins, just as the Scriptures said. He was buried, and he was raised from the dead on the third day, as the Scriptures said.[70]

---

[69] See also Acts 22:1–5.

[70] 1 Cor. 15:3–4, NLT.

The second reason Paul believes in the resurrection of Christ is that:

It fulfilled scriptural prophecy.

Everything that happened to Jesus—his death, his burial, and his resurrection on the third day—is in accordance with prophecies written hundreds of years earlier that we find in the Old Testament.

Since Paul was a Pharisee, well versed in the Old Testament Scripture,[71] he recognized Jesus as the Messiah to whom these Scriptures referred. Like Paul, Matthew also saw Jesus' ministry foretold by the Old Testament Prophets. Regarding Jesus' birth, Matthew begins his Gospel by writing:

All of this happened to fulfill the Lord's message
through his prophet.[72]
This is what the prophet wrote.[73]
This fulfilled what the Lord had spoken through the
prophet.[74]
This fulfilled the prophecy of Jeremiah.[75]
This fulfilled what was spoken by the prophets concerning
the Messiah.[76]
Isaiah had spoken of John when he said....[77]

Matthew and Paul believed that Jesus was the Messiah, and they believed that his resurrection, life, death and birth were

[71] Paul studied under Gamaliel who, according to Josephus, was one of the most notable Jewish scholars of his day—Acts 22:1–5.

[72] Matt. 1:22, NLT.

[73] Matt. 2:5, NLT.

[74] Matt. 2:15, NLT.

[75] Matt. 2:17, NLT.

[76] Matt. 2:23, NLT.

[77] Matt. 3:3, NLT.

foretold in the Scriptures. That is why Paul wrote, *Christ died for our sins, just as the Scriptures said. He was buried, and he was raised from the dead on the third day, as the Scriptures said.*[78]

The Third Reason Paul Believed Jesus Rose from the Dead

> *He was seen by Peter and then by the twelve apostles. After that, he was seen by more than five hundred of his followers at one time, most of whom are still alive, though some have died by now. Then he was seen by James and later by all the apostles.*[79]

The third reason Paul believed Jesus rose from the dead was because:

Many witnesses claimed to have seen the resurrected Christ.

After Jesus' tomb was found empty, he appeared to the disciples and to more than 500 other people. At the time Paul wrote these words, many of those eyewitnesses were still alive to verify what Paul was saying.

This is very different from the claims made by Islam and the Mormon Church. Both of these faiths' final testimony to truth (the Koran, for Muslims, and the Book of Mormon, for Mormons) is based upon the testimony of a single individual (Muhammad, for Muslims, and Joseph Smith, for Mormons). In both of those religions, faith has to be given to the hope that their one particular individual was correct.

The New Testament Scriptures are different. We have four Gospel accounts of Jesus' life—Matthew, Mark, Luke, and John. In addition to these, we have the writings of Paul, James, Peter, Jude, the unknown writer of Hebrews, and the Old Testament

---

[78] 1 Cor. 15:3–4, NLT.

[79] 1 Cor. 15:5–7, NLT.

Prophets. They all testify about Jesus and his resurrection. I would be suspicious if only one person wrote the Bible. Even Old Testament law requires more than one witness to judge a case: *One witness is not enough to convict a person accused of any crime or offense they may have committed. A matter must be established by the testimony of two or three witnesses.*[80]

Paul believed in the resurrection of Christ because it was based on the testimony of many credible witnesses.

The Fourth Reason Paul Believed Jesus Rose from the Dead

The fourth reason Paul believed Jesus rose from the dead was because:

He personally met and experienced the resurrected Jesus.

Last of all, I saw him, too, long after the others, as though I had been born at the wrong time.[81]

In Acts chapter nine, we read of Saul's (Paul's name before his conversion) trip to Damascus, where *Saul was uttering threats with every breath. He was eager to destroy the Lord's followers.*[82] On his way to this city, a bright light fell from heaven and blinded Paul, and he heard a voice that said, "*Saul, Saul, why are you persecuting me?*"

"*Who are you, Sir?*" Saul asked.

"*I am Jesus, the one you are persecuting.*"[83]

From that point on, Paul's life was never the same. Paul personally met the risen Lord. He had joined the ranks of eyewitnesses. This leads us to our fifth and final point for this chapter.

---

[80] Deut. 19:15, NLT.

[81] 1 Cor. 15:8, NLT.

[82] Acts 9:1, NLT.

[83] Acts 9:4–5, NLT.

The Fifth Reason Paul Believed
Jesus Rose from the Dead

Paul believed in the resurrected Jesus because:

He saw and experienced Jesus' power to change lives.

Speaking of his own life, Paul wrote:

For I am the least of all the apostles, and I am not worthy to be called an apostle after the way I persecuted the church of God. But whatever I am now, it is all because God poured out his special favor on me—and not without results. For I have worked harder than all the other apostles, yet it was not I but God who was working through me by his grace. So it makes no difference whether I preach or they preach. The important thing is that you believed what we preached to you.[84]

Paul realized that he didn't deserve God's grace. He was one who persecuted the Church, yet God still saw fit to not only save him, but to allow him to be an effective witness for his Kingdom.

Paul could say that he believed that "on the third day Jesus rose from the dead" because:

1. It is not something that he made up, but something he *received*.
2. It fulfilled prophecy and Scripture.
3. Many witnesses claimed to have seen the resurrected Christ.
4. He personally met and experienced the resurrected Jesus.
5. He saw and experienced Jesus' power to change lives.

We could go on and talk about other evidence, like the empty

---

[84] 1 Cor. 15:9–11, NLT.

tomb, the birth of the church, the silence of Jesus' enemies, and the accounts written outside of the Bible.[85]

Those who believe in the resurrection of Christ do not need to do so on a blind, irrational leap of faith. They can confidently put their faith in the highly reasonable and probable fact that Jesus rose from the dead. As the one writing this book, I also can tell you:

1. This is not a story I invented.
2. In my study of the Old Testament Scriptures, it appears that Jesus really did fulfill many prophecies written hundreds of years before he came in the flesh.
3. Today, many people *still* testify to having encountered Christ in their lives.
4. I have personally encountered Christ in my life.[86]
5. I can give countless stories of people whose lives have been changed because of Christ.

The Apostles' Creed states that; "On the third day Jesus rose from the dead." Or, in the words of Paul, *the fact is that Christ has been raised from the dead. He has become the first of a great harvest of those who will be raised to life again.*[87]

In the first few verses of first Corinthians, Paul says that it is *by this gospel* (that is, by the fact that Jesus came, lived, died, and rose again) that *we are saved.* This is not something that can only be acknowledged intellectually. We must surrender to Christ and his message. Jesus can give life because he is the one who has conquered death.

Becoming a Christian does not mean that we become perfect, but it *does* mean that a process of perfection begins in us. A new life

---

[85] If you are interested in doing more research, a good place to start is with the books mentioned in footnote sixty-seven.

[86] For c & d: Not necessarily in the same way as the New Testament eyewitness saw the risen Christ, but we still have had very specific Christ encounters.

[87] 1 Cor. 15:20, NLT.

starts growing as we start to become more like the human beings we were intended to be. This happens because, when we hand our life over to Christ, he gives us his Holy Spirit who empowers us to bring about these life changes.[88] Jesus rose from the dead and he can raise you from the dead as well—eternally as well as immediately.

> [Jesus said], *"I am the resurrection and the life. Those who believe in me, even though they die like everyone else, will live again. They are given eternal life for believing in me and will never perish. Do you believe this?"*[89]

---

[88] This will be discussed in greater detail in chapter seven.

[89] John 11:25–26, NLT.

chapter six

I Believe That Jesus Ascended into Heaven, and Sits on the Right Hand of God, the Father Almighty; He Will Come to Judge the Living and the Dead

A majority of people believe in life after death. According to studies done in Reginald Bibby's book, *Fragmented Gods,* close to seventy percent of Canadians believe in life after death, although their views on the afterlife are all over the map. Four out of ten Canadians said they believed there was something after death, but that they had no idea what it was going to be like.

Some of the following comments express this ambiguity: "As for heaven, hell, and purgatory, I probably will spend time in all three," claimed a sixty-three-year-old man from Charlottetown. A seventy-year-old housewife from Montreal said, "I would like to believe that there is such a thing as reincarnation, but who knows." A thirty-one-year-old from St. John's said, "There will be a resurrection and several degrees of heavens."[90]

---

[90] Reginald Bibby, *Fragmented Gods* (Toronto, ON: Irwin, 1987) pp. 66–67.

The pre-settlement Indian view of death seems appropriate for where many are at today. Diamond Jenness described it:

> Not for one moment did they believe that death put an end to all existence; but so dense a fog obscured the after-life, so conflicting were the opinions about it, that they planned their course for an earthly existence only and blindly resigned themselves to whatever fate awaited them hereafter.[91]

For this reason, even many of those who look forward to the afterlife do so with a fear of the unknown. As much as they anticipate it, they don't quite want to go there yet. The following joke pokes fun at this anxiety.

> Two guys are sitting down for a coffee and have the following conversation.
> "Well, I've got some good news and bad news in regards to some of your fears about heaven. Which would you like to hear first?"
> "Give me the good news."
> "Okay, I've discovered that there is going to be hockey in heaven."
> "That's great, but what is the bad news?"
> "The bad news is that your first game is tomorrow morning."

How do we know if there is an afterlife? What is this afterlife going to be like? Is there really a place called heaven, as is stated in the Apostles' Creed? How do we know if we are going to get there? Is Christ really going to come to this world again and judge all those living and all those who have died? How will I stand at this judgment?

To simply brush these questions aside because of the diversity of opinions does not solve the anxiety many Canadians live under. We may try and suppress our anxiety, and not think about these

---

91 *Ibid.*, p. 67.

"ultimate questions"—many attempt to do this through our cultural drug of staying busy. If we move fast enough, we just don't have time to *think*. The questions, however, don't go away. For some, it takes a crash, a breakdown, or a time staring up at a heart-monitor, for these questions to come flooding back.

The reason we cannot avoid thinking about these things is because it is part of our spiritual DNA. If we truly have been created by God, as was stated in chapter two, then it is natural for us to long for something bigger than what we can see and touch at this single moment in history.

It is no wonder that "national surveys have found that... some seven in ten [Canadians] report that they reflect on what happens after death, life's purpose, and whether or not there is a God or a Supreme Being."[92] Are these people neurotic, or are they expressing a longing that shows they inwardly know there is more to life than what tangibly meets the eye? It is natural and normal to be asking, "What is going to happen to me when I die? Is there more to life than this world we know? Is there really an afterlife?" In the Bible we read:

> *If Christ has not been raised, then your faith is useless, and you are still under condemnation for your sins. In that case, all who have died believing in Christ have perished! And if we have hope in Christ only for this life, we are the most miserable people in the world.*[93]

> *Let me tell you a wonderful secret God has revealed to us. Not all of us will die, but we will all be transformed. It will happen in a moment, in the blinking of an eye, when the last trumpet is blown. For when the trumpet sounds, the Christians who have died will be raised with transformed*

[92] *Ibid.*, p. 62.

[93] 1 Cor. 15:17–19, NLT.

bodies. And then we who are living will be transformed so that we will never die.[94]

According to the Scriptures, there *is* an afterlife. Let's unpack what the Bible teaches through the synopsis given to us in the Apostles' Creed:

"I believe that Jesus ascended into heaven, and sits on the right hand of God, the Father Almighty; from there He will come to judge the living and the dead."

Jesus Ascended into Heaven

Take a few moments now and read Acts 1:1–11. After Jesus' crucifixion and resurrection, we read that he showed himself to many people. He gave many convincing proofs that he was alive again. He appeared to people for a period of forty days, and continued to preach about the Kingdom of God. He promised his disciples the Holy Spirit. And, before his disciples' very eyes, he ascended into heaven. After Jesus had disappeared, and everyone was standing around looking into the sky, an angel appeared to them and said, *"Jesus has been taken away from you into heaven. And someday, just as you saw him go, he will return!"*[95]

One of the reasons we can know there is a heaven is because Jesus' story and message have proved trustworthy and, therefore, his teachings in this area should be given as much credit as the rest. The fact that Jesus came from heaven, went back to heaven, and will come again gives us a very reliable source regarding the fact of heaven. A chorus sung in some churches goes like this: "He came from heaven to earth, from the earth to the cross, from the cross to the grave, from the grave to the sky."

At this point, you may be saying, "Alright, I'm convinced that Jesus lived, taught, died, and even rose from the dead. There is no

---

[94] 1 Cor. 15:51–52, NLT.

[95] Acts 1:11, NLT.

reason for me to think he was wrong about heaven, but my question is: What is heaven *like*? Where is it? How do I get there? Do I *want* to get there?

When one of the first Russian astronauts arrived in space, he arrogantly looked outside his rocket and said something to the effect of, "Now I know there is no God, for here I am in the heavens and I don't see him anywhere."

The idea that heaven exists up in the sky and that hell is in the depths of the earth comes from the medieval idea of a tiered universe. Many of the paintings from that era depict the universe in layers, like an onion. These paintings correctly depict the concept of a world larger than we can see and touch. The problem comes when we comprehend these pictures as describing a scientific cosmology. The idea the painter was trying to get across should be affirmed as true, but that does not mean reality is exactly what we see in these paintings.

We need to be careful that we don't do the same thing with the Bible. The Bible uses words to paint pictures of heaven, in order to give us an understanding of this wonderful place where God and people will live together. We should not take the images of "streets paved with gold," and "walled cities,"[96] and even the pictures of hell as a "lake of fire" as literal, but as symbols.

When we read that Jesus *ascended* into heaven, we need to be careful to not assume that Jesus took a ride on a cloud spaceship. In Acts we read that Jesus was "taken up" before their eyes and a

---

[96] For instance, why would heaven look like a city from a certain era of history? Today great cities are not walled. Why should the heavenly city look like something from the Roman era? Also, gold streets would be worthless in a place where gold no longer has value. Gold is valuable for us now and walled cities were strong and well-protected in the Roman Empire. The point, however, that heaven is valuable, strong, and protected from its enemies is true. The gold and the walls are merely *symbols* of reality.

cloud hid him from their sight. Jesus was lifted into the air, as God often uses what we can understand, but as Jesus was hidden from their sight, he disappeared into the heavenly realm—he didn't ride a cloud to a place in outer space called heaven.

It is probably better to understand heaven and hell as existing in different dimensions rather than on different galactic levels. It is important to understand that there is a "here-and-now" heavenly and hellish realm, as well as a future heavenly and hellish world.[97] The Bible talks about angels and demons and powers all around us, even though we don't often see them. In the same way, atoms and molecules are all around us, and unless we have a special instrument, we cannot see them. The spectrum of colours is another example of that which extends far beyond what the human eye can pick up. This does not mean these other colours do not exist, but that they exist in a realm beyond the one we can see. In order to describe something beyond our understanding, we are limited to pictures from our world.

We can be sure the Bible teaches us about a place called heaven that is wonderful, good, eternal, and where people who have surrendered themselves to Christ will be in perfect fellowship with one another and with God. There is also a place called hell, where those who willfully choose to rebel against God will suffer eternal destruction and death.

Another truth we find about the afterlife or heavenly realm is that:

Jesus Sits on the Right Hand of God the Father Almighty.

Speaking of Christ's role in heaven today, God the Father said to his Son, *"Sit in honor at my right hand until I humble your enemies, making them a footstool under your feet."*[98]

---

[97] This means that Paradise (heaven) and the Lake of Fire (hell) do not currently exist filled with people. According to the Bible, these places are created after this age has ended. However, this does not deny that a heavenly angelic realm and a hellish demonic realm exist today. We will talk more about this future heaven and hell in chapter nine.

We need to be careful to understand the picture here. Jesus and his Father are not sitting on literal thrones, with Jesus putting his feet upon a literal coffee table his Father built for him out of his enemies. The things this symbolizes, however, are true. The picture of Jesus sitting at the right hand of his Father represents his authority. In ancient days, to be at the right hand of the king was to be the strength of the king and to share his authority.

We see a historical account of this when Joseph interpreted the dreams of Pharaoh and Pharaoh put Joseph next to him in command:

> *Then Pharaoh placed his own signet ring on Joseph's finger as a symbol of his authority. He dressed him in beautiful clothing and placed the royal gold chain about his neck. Pharaoh also gave Joseph the chariot of his second-in-command, and wherever he went the command was shouted, "Kneel down!" So Joseph was put in charge of all Egypt. And Pharaoh said to Joseph, "I am the king, but no one will move a hand or a foot in the entire land of Egypt without your approval."*[99]

Without Christ's word, the Father will not lift a hand or foot.[100] So, the picture of Jesus sitting at the right hand of God the Father shows Jesus as the one having authority over all things—*all things* meaning his enemies as well. *I make your enemies a footstool for your feet.*

It was a common practice for ancient conquerors to prostrate their enemies before them and put their feet on their necks to show their triumph. We see this practice in another historical account recorded in the Bible. After Joshua had conquered five Amorite kings, we read:

> *Then Joshua said, "Remove the rocks covering the opening of*

---

[98] Heb. 1:13, NLT.

[99] Gen. 41:42–44, NLT.

[100] God the Father having *hands* and *feet* is also merely a picture.

the cave and bring the five kings to me." So they brought the five kings out of the cave—the kings of Jerusalem, Hebron, Jarmuth, Lachish, and Eglon. Joshua told the captains of his army, "Come and put your feet on the kings' necks." And they did as they were told.
"Don't ever be afraid or discouraged," Joshua told his men. "Be strong and courageous, for the LORD is going to do this to all of your enemies." Then Joshua killed each of the five kings and hung them on five trees until evening.[101]

Many of us are uncomfortable with the aspects of Christ that don't fit our stereotype, but the Bible speaks, in many places, of him *conquering* his enemies. Speaking of the end of time, we read:

So the angel swung his sickle on the earth and loaded the grapes into the great winepress of God's wrath. And the grapes were trodden in the winepress outside the city, and blood flowed from the winepress in a stream about 180 miles long and as high as a horse's bridle.[102]

God warned Satan, after he deceived Adam and Eve in the garden, that the Messiah was going to come and crush his head.[103] Paul echoes this when he writes, *the God of peace will soon crush Satan under your feet.*[104]

The phrase, "Jesus sits on the right hand of God the Father Almighty," reminds us that he has the authority to rule over all things and will have victory over his enemies.

A third concept we learn from this stanza of the creed is that:

---

[101] Josh. 10:22–26, NLT.

[102] Rev. 14: 19–20, NLT.

[103] Gen. 3:15.

[104] Rom. 16:20, NLT.

Jesus Will Come Again

Jesus has been taken away from you into heaven. And someday, just as you saw him go, he will return![105]

In Christian circles, the second coming of Christ seems to continually be a popular rage—often to the embarrassment of thinking Christians. Walk into any Christian bookstore and you are bound to find fictional novels about the end (which never seem to end), comic books, CDs, DVDs, movies, and even videos you can leave behind for your loved ones who missed the train. All you would have had to do was look at the Y2K stuff on the discount shelf on January 1, 2000, to wish that some Christians would keep their mouths closed! There is nothing like incorrectly and continually predicting the end of the world to make Christianity look goofy. We all know the story of the boy who cried wolf! There was even a popular book out in the 1980s entitled *88 Reasons Why Christ Will Return in 1988*—whoops!

To anyone inquiring about the Christian faith, I can tell you these continual predictions are not what the Bible teaches. In fact, a case could be made that making end-times predictions is even unbiblical. Jesus taught us, *"The Father sets those dates and they are not for you to know."*[106]

The Apostle Paul wrote:

I really don't need to write to you about how and when all this will happen, dear brothers and sisters. For you know quite well that the day of the Lord will come unexpectedly, like a thief in the night.[107]

It is clear from Scripture that Christ will come again, and that

---

[105] Acts 1:11, NLT.

[106] Acts 1:7, NLT.

[107] 1 Thess. 5:1–2, NLT.

this age will come to an end. We cannot ignore this. It is the *when* that the Bible does not give us specific details on. In describing that last day, Paul writes:

> *For the Lord himself will come down from heaven with a commanding shout, with the call of the archangel, and with the trumpet call of God. First, all the Christians who have died will rise from their graves. Then, together with them, we who are still alive and remain on the earth will be caught up in the clouds to meet the Lord in the air and remain with him forever. So comfort and encourage each other with these words.*[108]

He Will Come to Judge the Living and the Dead

When Christ comes again, it will happen on a historical day with people still alive on the earth. At that time, all those who have passed away before this Second Coming will be brought back to life. The followers of Christ will be rewarded with eternal life in heaven and those who have chosen against God will experience eternal death in hell.

> *And I saw a great white throne, and I saw the one who was sitting on it. The earth and sky fled from his presence, but they found no place to hide. I saw the dead, both great and small, standing before God's throne. And the books were opened, including the Book of Life. And the dead were judged according to the things written in the books, according to what they had done.*[109]

When this verse teaches that they will be judged *according to what they had done*, we need to understand that it must be referring to what they had done *with Christ*—because we know from other

---

108 1 Thess. 4:16–18, NLT.

109 Rev. 20:11–12, NLT.

places in Scripture that it is not by our good works that we earn a place in heaven.[110]

Not everyone will be in heaven. Those who reject Christ will be judged and conquered by him, while those who receive Christ will be rewarded by him and share in his victory.

God does not delight in punishing people, but he does give them free choice. For those who have never heard the gospel, we simply don't know their fate. To those who have heard, he would be an unjust God if he did not give them the choice to accept or reject him. The natural consequences of eternity without the life-giving God, however, can only be death.

Because of this, God raised him up to the heights of heaven and gave him a name that is above every other name, so that at the name of Jesus every knee will bow, in heaven and on earth and under the earth, and every tongue will confess that Jesus Christ is Lord, to the glory of God the Father. Therefore God exalted him to the highest place and gave him the name that is above every name, that at the name of Jesus every knee should bow, in heaven and on earth and under the earth, and every tongue confess that Jesus Christ is Lord, to the glory of God the Father.[111]

"I Believe that Jesus ascended into heaven, and sits on the right hand of God the Father Almighty; from there He will come to judge the living and the dead."

When we understand this, it should cause us to be ready and to live holy and purposeful lives—which can only *really* happen through a relationship with Christ.

Without wavering, let us hold tightly to the hope we say we have, for God can be trusted to keep his promise. Think of

---

[110] Eph. 2:8.

[111] Phil. 2:9–11, NLT.

ways to encourage one another to outbursts of love and good deeds. And let us not neglect our meeting together, as some people do, but encourage and warn each other, especially now that the day of his coming back again is drawing near.

Dear friends, if we deliberately continue sinning after we have received a full knowledge of the truth, there is no other sacrifice that will cover these sins. There will be nothing to look forward to but the terrible expectation of God's judgment and the raging fire that will consume his enemies. Anyone who refused to obey the law of Moses was put to death without mercy on the testimony of two or three witnesses. Think how much more terrible the punishment will be for those who have trampled on the Son of God and have treated the blood of the covenant as if it were common and unholy. Such people have insulted and enraged the Holy Spirit who brings God's mercy to his people.

For we know the one who said, "I will take vengeance. I will repay those who deserve it."

He also said, "The Lord will judge his own people."

It is a terrible thing to fall into the hands of the living God.[112]

---

[112] Heb. 10: 23–31, NLT.

chapter seven

I Believe in the Holy Spirit

Christians, like Jews and Muslims, believe in one God, and yet, unlike Jews and Muslims, they believe that the Father is God, the Son is God, and the Spirit is God. This concept, eventually described by the early church as "the Trinity," is essential to understanding the character of God, though beyond our limited mathematical and logical understanding of reality. The Bible tells us there is only one God; however, the Father, the Son, and the Holy Spirit are separate persons, each possessing the full qualities of divinity.[113] What are we to do with such an apparent contradiction?

We must never write off a concept about God simply because we cannot understand it. It should not be a surprise that when we are speaking about God, there are going to be things beyond our comprehension.

---

[113] We have already seen this in the earlier chapters regarding the Father and the Son, and will deal with the Holy Spirit in this current chapter.

C.S. Lewis reminds us that the world we see and touch may not be all there is. To describe this, he gives the example of a couple of individuals living in a two-dimensional world, both of whom have never known anything but a two dimensional world. One day they come upon a square and both agree, with all their great rational faculties, that it consists of four sides—no more and no less.

Suddenly, another person joins the conversation, claiming to be from another world/dimension—the third! This person claims that the object they are looking at has six sides (a cube). The individuals who only understand two dimensions look at the one from the third dimension as if he were crazy and downright foolish.

Lewis states that many *seeming* contradictions about God that we find in the Bible are like this example—they describe a being from another dimension that we only have a certain capacity to understand. The Trinity is one such concept.

The Trinity reveals to us the character of God, and, in turn, gives us a standard for ethics. When Jesus said that the greatest commandment was to love God and to love one another,[114] he was not just pulling a concept out of the air. God is love[115] because God existed eternally in a love relationship as Father, Son, and Spirit. Loving God and loving one another is the standard of all ethics for the very reason that it stems from who God is. If God had existed solo, he could not *be* love. Love would be an afterthought, for love would only have come into being *after* God had created something to love.

God was not lonely or lacking anything before he created. He was complete as pure community and love. From this eternal foundation, all ethics find their standard. There is one[116] God[117]

---

114 Mark 12:28–34.

115 1 John 4:8.

116 One is also understood to mean unified, not just singular. For example; when Adam and Eve came together they became one/unified (Gen. 2:24).

117 Mark 12:29.

existing as three perfectly united persons in the Father,[118] the Son,[119] and the Holy Spirit.[120] These three persons perfectly love each other, have perfect communication, were all involved in building a perfect creation, and even after humanity sinned, became involved in the perfect plan of redemption.

Now, let's look at the person of the Holy Spirit, to whom this stanza of the Creed refers.

I Believe in the Holy Spirit

Who is the Holy Spirit? What does the Holy Spirit do? What does it mean for a person or a church to be Spirit-filled? To begin with, take your Bible and read John 16:5–15, where Jesus talks about the Holy Spirit. We will use this text as our basis for this chapter.

The Holy Spirit is a Person

Jesus does not refer to the Holy Spirit as a force, power, or energy, but as a personal being. Jesus calls the Holy Spirit a "he," not an "it." We have no reason to read into this text that Jesus is merely personifying the Holy Spirit. The fact that the Holy Spirit is referred to with a personal pronoun, and that elsewhere in the Bible, we find the Holy Spirit can be grieved,[121] has a will, can think,[122] speaks,[123] and takes on many other personal qualities, makes it clear that the Bible presents the Holy Spirit as a divine, rational, personal being. The question that then follows is, "What does the Holy Spirit do?"

---

[118] Matt. 6:9.

[119] John 1:1–5 and 14.

[120] Acts 5:2–4.

[121] Eph. 4:30.

[122] Acts 15:28.

[123] Acts 1:16.

The Holy Spirit's Work in the Believer: The Counselor

In John 16:7, Jesus says that when he goes away, he will send the Holy Spirit—whom he refers to as "the Counselor." Today, the word "counselor" conjures up images of a person lying on a couch spilling their emotions to a psychologist sitting in a chair listening and writing on a clipboard. That, I assure you, is not the biblical idea of what is meant by counselor!

The Holy Spirit is not our personal therapist. The counselor role that the Holy Spirit plays is closer to that of a mentor, a coach, or a teacher. When we surrender our lives to Christ, God's Holy Spirit comes alongside of us to mentor, coach, and teach us in the ways of Christ. This is exactly why those individuals who want to get to a certain level of goodness, or arrive at a certain point in their life before they come to Christ, have it backwards. It is like trying to put on your socks *after* you have your shoes on! If we recognize and believe in Christ and his message, we need to surrender our lives to him first; then the Holy Spirit is given to us as a Counselor to help us become like Christ.

Jesus said that the Holy Spirit

> *...will guide you into all truth. He will not be presenting his own ideas; he will be telling you what he has heard. He will tell you about the future. He will bring me glory by revealing to you whatever he receives from me. All that the Father has is mine; this is what I mean when I say that the Spirit will reveal to you whatever he receives from me.*[124]

The moment we become Christians, we are given the Holy Spirit as a gift to guide, empower, and teach us the truth of God's Word.

The Holy Spirit does this by counseling us in understanding Scripture.

The Holy Spirit does not speak contrary to, or over and above,

---

[124] John 16:13–15, NLT.

Scripture—rather, he works alongside of Scripture. *He will not be presenting his own ideas; he will be telling you what he has heard.* No individual can ever claim to speak a "word" from the Spirit and contradict what the Bible teaches.

The Bible is God's written Word; therefore, if the Holy Spirit teaches and confirms what he hears God speaking, it will always be in accordance with his written Word. When we read our Bibles and open our hearts to God, we can be assured that the Holy Spirit will speak to us. John Stott wrote,

> To use the Holy Spirit to rationalize our laziness is nearer blasphemy than piety… Trust in the Holy Spirit must not be used as a device to save us the labor of Biblical and contemporary studies.[125]

The Holy Spirit also coaches us in prayer.

Paul writes:

> *The Holy Spirit helps us in our distress. For we don't even know what we should pray for, nor how we should pray. But the Holy Spirit prays for us with groanings that cannot be expressed in words. And the Father who knows all hearts knows what the Spirit is saying, for the Spirit pleads for us believers in harmony with God's own will.*[126]

This is not an excuse for laziness in our prayer life, either, although it is a great assurance to know that the Holy Spirit prays alongside of us in a way beyond what we are able. In some instances, this manifests in what has been called "tongues":

> *For if your gift is the ability to speak in tongues, you will be talking to God but not to people, since they won't be able to*

---

[125] John Stott, *Christian Mission* (Downers Grove, Illinois, IVP, 1975) p. 127.

[126] Rom. 8:26–27, NLT.

understand you. You will be speaking by the power of the Spirit, but it will all be mysterious.[127]

In the Bible, we seem to have two kinds of supernatural tongues. One type is found in Acts 2, when the Holy Spirit comes upon the followers of Jesus and they suddenly speak in an earthly language they had not previously learned. This enabled them to present the gospel to people in their own languages.

The second kind of supernatural tongue, found in 1 Corinthians 14, appears to be the Holy Spirit speaking to and interceding on our, and/or the Church's, behalf. The Spirit does this by using our voices in a mysterious, unearthly language. Both of these tongues are biblical, connected with the Holy Spirit, and we are given guidelines in their use. It is unwise to deny their reality simply because we may find them strange.

Some churches, however, have incorrectly taught that every Christian should speak in tongues as a *sign* that the Holy Spirit lives in them. This is wrong for a couple of reasons. First, the Bible clearly teaches that only *some* Christians will speak in tongues—not all.[128] Second, as we are going to see later in this chapter, the *sign* of the Holy Spirit is not found in gifts and talents, but in a growing Christ-likeness of character.[129] In the same way, the *sign* of a Spirit-filled church is not a gifted church, but a church that reflects Christ's character.

When we surrender our life to Christ and start living for him, and when we get into the Bible and start praying,

The Holy Spirit works alongside us to produce Christ-like fruit.

Paul writes:

When the Holy Spirit controls our lives, he will produce this

---

[127] 1 Cor. 14:2, NLT.

[128] 1 Cor. 12 (see especially verses 10, 19, 27–31).

[129] Gal. 5:22–25.

kind of fruit in us: love, joy, peace, patience, kindness, goodness,
faithfulness, gentleness, and self-control. Here there is no conflict
with the law.
Those who belong to Christ Jesus have nailed the passions and
desires of their sinful nature to his cross and crucified them there.
If we are living now by the Holy Spirit, let us follow the Holy
Spirit's leading in every part of our lives. Let us not become con-
ceited, or irritate one another, or be jealous of one another.[130]

A spirit-filled individual and a spirit-filled church is one where *love,*
joy, peace, patience, kindness, goodness, faithfulness, gentleness and self-
control are growing and evident.

The Holy Spirit empowers us to love each other, forgive people
when we've been wronged, and be joyful when other people suc-
ceed. Spirit-filled people stand up for what is right and holy, but
they are not argumentative and divisive. They strive to be peace-
makers, and are patient with each other's shortcomings. They are
kind towards outsiders and individuals who are different. They
strive for moral goodness in every area of their lives. Spirit-filled
people are faithful in their marriages, their friendships, and their
stewardship. They are gentle in the way they treat people they don't
agree with. They are self-controlled with the use of their tongue,
and don't lash out or spread gossip.

This is what it means to be like Christ, and this can only
develop in a person *after* receiving Christ and being given the Holy
Spirit. Only through daily submission to the Spirit of God can
these things become a reality in our lives. That is why Jesus said it
is the Holy Spirit who guides into all truth.[131]

Another way the Holy Spirit counsels us, which relates to the last
point, is that he produces unity among believers.

---

[130] Gal. 5:22–26, NLT.

[131] John 16:13.

If Christians truly *do* begin to live in the power of the Holy Spirit, it is only natural that they would live in unity. Paul encouraged the Church to live like this when he wrote:

> *I, a prisoner for serving the Lord, beg you to lead a life worthy of your calling, for you have been called by God. Be humble and gentle. Be patient with each other, making allowance for each other's faults because of your love. Always keep yourselves united in the Holy Spirit, and bind yourselves together with peace.*[132]

God's Spirit calls and enables the Church to live in unity. Not uniformity, but unity. There is great room for diversity in the Church. This diversity, however, enacts itself in unity. The body is made up of many parts, but they all work together as one.

Just as we began this chapter discussing the nature and character of God, we now find the call to be a diverse, but unified, Church reflected in the diverse, but unified, God. Paul calls the Church to keep *united in the Holy Spirit*. By doing this, we grow in Christ-likeness, as we learn to be humble, gentle, patient, and loving towards one other.

The Holy Spirit's Work in Unbelievers: The Convictor

The Holy Spirit also convicts non-Christians by working alongside of Christians to share God's story with them.

When Jesus promised the Holy Spirit to his followers, he said:

> *But when the Holy Spirit has come upon you, you will receive power and will tell people about me everywhere—in Jerusalem, throughout Judea, in Samaria, and to the ends of the earth.*[133]

---

132 Eph. 4:1–3, NLT.

133 Acts 1:8, NLT.

When Christians live in a Spirit-filled way, in unity, and according to the fruits of the Spirit, their message becomes very attractive to unbelievers. The unbeliever will experience the true Christian message by the Church's love. The Holy Spirit works in the life of an unbeliever not as a counselor, but as one who *convicts*. In explaining this, Jesus said:

> And when he comes, he will convince the world of its sin, and of God's righteousness, and of the coming judgment. The world's sin is unbelief in me.[134]

The Holy Spirit convicts people of their sin with the intent of helping them see their need for Christ.

The Holy Spirit's job, for both the believer and the unbeliever, is to draw people into an ongoing, deepening relationship with Christ. When individuals and churches allow this to happen, the world sees Jesus with increasing clarity.

> A church in whose preaching there is the authority of the Spirit, in whose worship there is the joy of the Spirit, in whose fellowship there is the love of the Spirit, and in whose service the gifts of the Spirit are in full use—such a church will witness to Christ just by being itself. It will convey to others that Jesus is alive and sharing his life with his people.[135]

---

[134] John 16:8–9, NLT.

[135] Robin Keeley (Ed), *Exploring Christian Faith* (Nashville, TN: Nelson, 1982) p. 251; Tom Smail, "Life in the Holy Spirit."

chapter eight

I Believe in the Holy Christian Church, the Communion of Saints and the Forgiveness of Sins

It is a popular cliché for people today to say that they are "into spirituality, but not organized religion," or that they are "interested in Jesus, but not the Church." I have had a number of conversations like this, even from people who claim to be Christians. One man I talked to went so far as to say that the Church stifled his relationship with Christ by giving him an inaccurate picture of Jesus. The interesting thing was that the more he and I talked the more it came out that he also had a selective view of Jesus. Anything Jesus said that he was uncomfortable with was something, he figured, the Church added.

We in the Western world have been taught to compartmentalize our lives. Someone can be immoral in his or her private life, and people feel this should have no bearing on their public or professional life. Politicians can abuse alcohol and be unfaithful to their spouses, but as long as they keep that in the private realm, many people feel they can still govern the country and put just laws in place. Teachers can read and view child pornography, as long as it is done in the privacy of their own homes and "no one gets hurt," and people feel they can still entrust their children to that person. We have done the same nonsense with our spiritual beliefs.

"Religion," we are told, is an individual's private matter—spiritual beliefs are one's own business and should not affect the way a person does his or her job or lives in public. To question or challenge someone's personal view has also become taboo.[136] These are self-contradictory, but no one seems to notice. If my personal view allows my religion to affect my public life, it should be taboo for anyone to challenge it.

Pushing faith into a private affair is a huge factor in why so many Canadians claim to believe in a god or a supernatural power, and yet so few regularly attend a church, synagogue, temple, or mosque. Religion has lost its public/community aspect.

When it comes to true Christianity, pure individuality is impossible. We cannot put our faith into a compartment disconnected from the rest of life. Personal faith, the world in which we live, and a local community of believers, all come under the lordship of Christ.

The God of the Bible, who in his very nature *is* community—and who taught us that love for him and one another is a summary of life's purpose—cannot be followed and worshipped solo. Jesus taught that he was going to build his church;[137] therefore, those

---

136 Anyone who knows basic philosophy and logic should be able to see the danger of this. Socrates, in many ways the catalyst of philosophy, built his whole system of thought on questioning everything. When we don't enter into debate, argument, challenge and dialogue we end up having a very superficial understanding of different ideas, as well as our own ideas. This holds true for every realm, including spirituality and religion. If Christianity is true, or if any other religious system is true (including a personal one that an individual may have made up by selecting ideas from various other belief systems), it should be able to stand up under challenge. Christians, as well as everyone else, need to be open to changing their ideas if they are discovered to be incorrect. A society that takes this freedom away, under the guise of tolerance, moves backward, not forward.

who believe that Jesus simply came to build them up individually are really living pseudo-Christianity. It is like saying you are a hockey player when you've never played for a team.

In Matthew's Gospel, Jesus is recorded as saying, *"And I tell you that you are Peter, and on this rock I will build my church, and the gates of Hell will not overcome it."* We should agree it was Jesus who started the Church. If we believe that God is a God of love, who calls us to love even to the point of forgiveness, then we see the need for the Church. Love and forgiveness can only be given and received in community.

When we realize that most of the New Testament letters are written in regards to *how* to be a church community, then we must agree that the Church, the community of saints, and the forgiveness of sins, as stated in the creed, have their origin at the very beginning of Christianity. You cannot accept the perfect Christ without also accepting the perfect, *but not yet* perfect, Church.

The Holy Christian Church, The Communion of Saints and the Forgiveness of Sins

Jesus called into being, believed in, and loved the holy Christian Church. In the Bible, we have many different pictures of the Church: "The Bride of Christ,"[138] "The Body of Christ,"[139] "God's flock,"[140] "God's chosen people," "God's Royal priesthood," "God's holy nation," "A people belonging to God,"[141] among a number of other names.

The question must be asked—"Can a person become a Christian, receive the Holy Spirit, and not be a part of the "Bride of Christ" and the "Body of Christ" as well as the other descriptions of the Church?" The answer is *no*!

---

[137] Matt. 16:18.

[138] Rev. 21:2.

[139] 1 Cor. 12.

[140] 1 Pet. 5:2.

[141] All in 1 Pet. 2:9.

Some Christians will try to get around this by saying that they are part of the *universal* Church[142] and, therefore, do not need to be part of a *local* church. While it is true that believers are part of the universal Church, they also need to be involved in a local church.

Paul deals with specific local churches in his letters. One cannot be a part of the universal Church if they do not learn how to be involved in a church on a local level. That is like claiming to love humanity, but not loving any specific individuals. Or, it is like saying that you have a concern for world poverty, but not helping a single poor family or individual. Those who love individuals and those who help a poor family are the ones who love humanity and have a concern for poverty. In the same way, those true Christians involved in a local church are the ones who are a part of the universal Church.

Connecting With a Church Keeps Us Alive

One reason why it is important to be part of a church is because the Church is the "Body of Christ," and we, as 1 Corinthians 12 says, are one part of the body and need each other. A hand, a finger, or a foot not connected to the body quickly loses its life.

If you have ever seen a daddy-long-legs spider lose one of its legs, you would have seen the leg twitch for a while and then lose its life. When a farmer chops the head off a chicken, the body flaps around for a few moments and then falls to the ground and dies. These disturbing scenes (for city slickers!) depict exactly what happens to us when we choose to *chop ourselves off* from the body of Christ. That is why Jesus said,

> *Yes, I am the vine; you are the branches. Those who remain in me, and I in them, will produce much fruit. For apart from me you can do nothing.*[143]

---

142 This refers to all true believers in Christ all over the world and all throughout time.

143 John 15:5, NLT.

Paul teaches in 1 Corinthians 12 that Christ is the head of the body. All the parts must be connected to the head, and none of the parts can say to any of the other parts, "I don't need you." The body is an interconnected unit, ultimately connected to Christ as head. A Christian who is not part of Christ's body at a local and universal level is a dead Christian.

Connecting With a Church Teaches Us to Love and Forgive

When we become Christians, we enter into a relationship with God and a new relationship with one another. Jesus stated:

> *The most important commandment is this: "Hear, O Israel! The Lord our God is the one and only Lord. And you must love the Lord your God with all your heart, all your soul, all your mind, and all your strength." The second is equally important: "Love your neighbor as yourself." No other commandment is greater than these.*[144]

To be born into Christ means to be born into a community where love and forgiveness are learned. God has declared the Church, as well as the individual Christian, perfect. That is why it is called the community of *saints*. The Church, like the individual Christian, however, is still *not yet* perfect, and is being sanctified by the work of the Holy Spirit.

Those believers who choose to reject the Church on the basis of her imperfection are denying the "perfect *but not yet*" reality of their own condition. The fact that the Church is declared perfect *but not yet* is no excuse for allowing blatant sin to continue in her midst. The Church is to live in Godly integrity while practicing love and forgiveness when members fail and, in cases where members are unrepentant, practice church discipline. The Church's condition of being *not yet* perfect makes her the ideal environment for learning and experiencing love and forgiveness.

---

[144] Mark 12:30–31, NLT.

The Apostles' Creed states that Christians believe "in the forgiveness of sins," but some Christians want a perfect church where they won't have to practice it! Maybe part of the reason God leaves the Church imperfect for a time is that he wants us to put what we say we believe into practice.

People are happy to hear that Jesus died for their sins, but forget Jesus taught that receiving his forgiveness includes extending forgiveness to others. Jesus died so we could pray, *"Forgive us our sins, just as we have forgiven those who have sinned against us."*[145] Forgiveness hurts because it means accepting the wrong done to us without holding a grudge or seeking vengeance. It would be foolish to think that it didn't hurt God to forgive us—just look at the cross. In an imperfect Church filled with imperfect Christians, we learn how to love and forgive as Christ did.

This topic of forgiveness always reminds me of the true story told by Corrie ten Boom, who was sent to a German concentration camp during WWII for hiding Jews in her house. I will let her tell it in her own words:

> It was in a church in Munich that I saw him.... One moment I saw the overcoat and the brown hat; the next, a blue uniform and a visored cap with its skull and crossbones. It came back with a rush: the huge room with its harsh overhead lights; the pathetic pile of dresses and shoes in the center of the floor; the shame of walking naked past this man.
>
> It was [now] 1947 and I had come from Holland to defeated Germany with the message that God forgives. "When we confess our sins," I said, "God casts them into the deepest ocean, gone forever."
>
> Now he was in front of me, hand thrust out: "A fine message."
>
> I fumbled in my pocketbook rather than take his hand.... He did not remember me.
>
> "Since (the war)," he went on, "I have become a Christian. I

---

145 Matt. 6:12; See also the Parable of the Unmerciful Servant in Matt. 18:23–35.

know that God has forgiven me for the cruel things I did, but I would like to hear it from your lips as well"—again the hand came out—"will you forgive me?" It could not have been many seconds that he stood there—hand held out—but to me it seemed hours as I wrestled with the most difficult thing I ever had to do; but I had to do it.... Forgiveness is an act of the will... I prayed silently. "I can lift my hand. I can do that much. You supply the feeling."

And so woodenly, mechanically, I thrust my hand into the one stretched out to me. And as I did, an incredible thing took place. The current started in my shoulder, raced down my arm, sprang into our joined hands. And then this healing warmth seemed to flood my whole being, bringing tears to my eyes.

"'I forgive you, brother!" I cried. "With all my heart."

I realized it was not my love. I had tried, and did not have the power. It was the power of the Holy Spirit.[146]

"I believe in the forgiveness of sins" means that the "community of saints" forgives one another. That is a huge aspect of being "the holy Christian Church."

What are the Basic Elements of a True Church?

Eugene Peterson wrote:

In worship the community of God's people assemble to hear God's word spoken in scripture, sermon, and sacrament.... At no time has there ever been a biblical faith, or any kind of continuing life in relation to God, apart from such common worship. By persisting in the frequent, corporate worship in which God's word is central, God's people are prevented from making up a religion out of their own private ideas of God. They are also prevented from making a private, individualized salvation out of what they experience, separating themselves from brothers and

---

[146] Os Guinness (Ed.), *Steering Through Chaos* (Colorado Springs, CO: NavPress, 2000) p. 301–303.

sisters with whom God has made it clear his saving love is to be shared, both in receiving and giving.[147]

To believe in the Church is to actively participate in it, just as to believe in Christ is to actively participate in a relationship with him. This happens when we give our lives over to Christ, connect with a local church, and learn to love and forgive one another. It is important, however, that we connect with a biblical church—for many false groups call themselves churches. In Acts 2:41,42, we find the basic components of a true church. Many churches do more than what is listed here, and that is all right, but no true church can do less, or be contrary to what we find recorded about the earliest description of the Church in history.

Those who believed what Peter said were baptized and added to the church—about three thousand in all. They joined with the other believers and devoted themselves to the apostles' teaching and fellowship, sharing in the Lord's Supper and in prayer.[148]

The five components of a true church are as follows:[149]

1. Evangelism

---

[147] Eugene Peterson, *Five Smooth Stones* (Grand Rapids, MI: Eerdmans, 1980) p. 18.

[148] Acts 2:41,42, NLT.

[149] It is interesting to note, in our day of extreme devotion to music, that you can have no music in church and still be a true church. A danger we run into in many churches today is that we lack the ability to spend quality time in learning the Apostles' teaching, in fellowship, in prayer, and in communion, because we spend so much of our time together singing and/or listening to music. Having music in a church service is not unbiblical, and can be a good tool for teaching and bringing people together, but it should never become the central component, or take up the most time, of a church service —this goes for *any* style of music. It is unfortunate that many people choose a church based on its music rather than on the five pillars mentioned in Acts 2:41,42.

2. Devotion to the Apostles' Teaching
3. Fellowship
4. Sharing in the Lord's Supper
5. Prayer

When a church is sharing the faith with others, teaching God's Word (the teachings of the Apostles), loving, forgiving, and caring for one another (fellowship), sharing in the Lord's Supper, and praying, that church becomes the strongest witness for Christ in the world.

The Church is not an organization, although her people do organize themselves. The Church is not a building, although most churches meet in buildings. The Church is not a particular Christian denomination, although most churches are a part of a denomination. The Church is a community of saints striving to live out Acts 2:41,42.

Evangelism

When trying to find a good church, you want to find one that strives to share the message of Christ with people who don't know Christ. In the Acts passage, we find Peter sharing his faith and a large group of individuals becoming believers and being added to the Church. The sign of these people's commitment was symbolized in their water baptism.

Baptism has been, and continues to be, practiced in different forms by different churches. Adult believer's baptism is done after a person has made a commitment to Christ and is usually enacted through fully immersing someone in and out of water, or through pouring water over them. Full immersion symbolizes that a person has died to their old life and been raised new into a life with Christ and is now entering the community of the Church. The act of pouring symbolizes that a person's sins have been washed away, they have been anointed as a child of God, and they are entering into the life of the Church.

Infant baptism is done on children before they are able to make a faith commitment. It is a covenantal promise that believing parents make over their child, which the child either affirms or rejects after being raised and trained in the faith of the Church. The children's acceptance of the Christian faith and their baptism is called confirmation. At that point, they become full members of the Church, and without it, their baptism is meaningless.

Baptism is a tangible sign intimately connected with evangelism. Upon the public profession of a person's faith before a body of believers, they are either baptized or they affirm their infant baptism. A healthy church is one that shares Christ with those who don't know him, gives people opportunities to receive Christ, and baptizes people as a sign of God's work in the lives of individuals.

Devotion to the Apostles' Teaching

When trying to find a good church, you want to find one that teaches and preaches from the Bible in their services and programs, and one that encourages their people to study, learn, mature, and teach others God's message.

Fellowship

When trying to connect with a good church, you want to find one that provides opportunities for interpersonal relationships to grow and develop, one that cares for the poor and those in need, and one that allows you to get involved according to your gifts.

Sharing in the Lord's Supper

In finding a good church, you want one that keeps Christ and his work at the center of everything it says and does. Sharing in the Lord's Supper, on a regular basis, is a key way that Christ asked us to continually remember him. Through this meal we symbolically show that we stand together as a community, because Christ gave up his body (bread) and blood (wine) so that we could be forgiven.

By eating and drinking Christ's body and blood, we show that we have taken him into our life. The Lord's Supper is not meant to be an end in itself, but a tangible reminder for us that Christ is the church's foundation.[150]

Prayer

In choosing a good church, you want to find one that believes in prayer and spends time worshiping God, listening to him, and communicating with him before, during, and after everything it does.

Conclusion

A healthy church is involved in more areas than these, but these five pillars in Acts 2:41, 42 are the bare minimum of a true church.[151] No church will do these things to perfection, but a

---

[150] The Holy Spirit is important and needs to be emphasized and taught in the church. However, the Holy Spirit should never be the *center* of the church's emphasis (as he is in some churches). The Holy Spirit's job is to lead us to Christ, not to himself—John 16:12–15. God the Father is also essential, but once again, we only have access to the Father *through* the Son. The Son, the cross, and his resurrection are the entry point to everything else. Because our heavenly Father loves us he points us to his Son— John 3:16. In truth, all persons of the Trinity point to each other. Only through the Son, however, do we receive the Holy Spirit and enter into a parent/child relationship with our heavenly Father. The central message of the church should be the same as Paul's, when he wrote: *"For I decided to concentrate only on Jesus Christ and his death on the cross."* (1 Cor. 2:2, NLT).

[151] Churches attempt to make their communities a better place to live, advocate for morality, and involve themselves in numerous other ministries. In everything they do, however, evangelism, the Bible, fellowship, Christ, communion and prayer are the base and must never be lost sight of. Examples of some different types of church ministries: Children, teens, parents, elderly, deaf, blind, single parents, widows, street children, building houses, restoring cars, classes, community events, political activism, working with refugees—the list is endless.

church that is continually striving to go back to these foundations is one that you would be wise to join.

To believe in Christ is to believe in the Church. When one surrenders his or her life to Christ, the Holy Spirit calls that person to connect with a local church in order to live and grow in the love and forgiveness taught in the gospel. Christians are people who say they believe, through their words and their actions, in "the holy Christian Church, the communion of saints, and the forgiveness of sins." Christians can also have the utmost confidence that the true Church will prevail, because Jesus said, *"I will build my church, and all the powers of hell will not conquer it."*[152]

---

[152] Matt. 16:18, NLT.

chapter nine

I Believe in the Resurrection of the Body and Life Everlasting

What happens to a person when they die? Nearly all world religions and ideologies attempt to answer this question. Even though many people today try to say all beliefs are basically the same, the reality is there are about as many different attempted answers to this question about death as belief systems.

Buddhism promises *nirvana*—a place where individuality ceases to exist and you become one with the great cosmic force, or energy, or mind of the universe. Mormons promise their men a planet of which they will become the god. Islamic suicide bombers (in some branches of Islam) are promised a harem of perpetual virgins for their supposed "martyrdom."

The ancient Egyptians, known for their embalming and mummification practices of dead bodies, believed that the souls of the dead temporarily departed and made habitation in birds. This soul would return to the old body only if it was in a good state of preservation. If the body was allowed to decay, the soul could not return and would dissolve into nothingness. For this reason, the Egyptians attempted to master the art of embalming. In fact, they did such a good job that we still have the corpse of Ramses II, who lived and ruled Egypt 3200 years ago! You can still see his facial features and skin on his face.

Some philosophers took a more hopeless view of death. The Greek thinker Aeschylus wrote, "When the dust drinks up a man's blood, there is no resurrection." Thomas Hobbes penned, "When I die the worms will devour my body, and I will commit myself to the great 'Perhaps.'" How about the words of the famous twentieth-century atheist and existential philosopher Jean Paul Sartre, who said, "Death is the final conversion. After death, there is nothing more to be decided. A person is all past. Present and future are no more."[153]

In contrast to these philosophers, the Apostle Paul wrote, *For to me, living is for Christ, and dying is even better.*[154] *O death, where is your victory? O death, where is your sting?*[155]

We could go on describing the different cultural beliefs and individual philosophies of people around the world and throughout history regarding the afterlife. The question "What happens to a person when they die?" is a universal one, because according to scientific and sociological studies, ten out of ten people die. So, what *does* happen to a person when they die? Why does Paul seem to speak with such confidence about death? Why and on what basis has the Church, throughout the ages, been able to say, "I believe in the resurrection of the body and the life everlasting"?

Jesus Did It!

One of the main reasons we can believe in the resurrection of the dead is because *Jesus rose from the dead.* As discussed in chapter

---

153 The origin of this Sartre quote is unknown to the author. If anyone recognizes it and knows the source, please do not hesitate to contact the author.

154 Phil. 1:21, NLT.

155 1 Cor. 15:55, NLT.

five, we found good evidence to believe that Jesus really did rise from the dead. Because of Jesus' resurrection, Paul could write, *Christ was raised first; then when Christ comes back, all his people will be raised.*[156] *The last enemy to be destroyed is death. For the Scriptures say, 'God has given him authority over all things.*[157] Because of Christ's resurrection, we can say, "I believe in the resurrection of the body and the life everlasting." There still are questions, however. Two that we will look at in the remainder of this chapter are:

1. What will we be like when we are resurrected?
2. When will our resurrection take place?

Ultimately these questions, when it comes to specific details, have to be left to mystery. The Bible does not give many clear descriptions of the afterlife. There are some things, however, the Bible does shed light on and so we will look at those.

The early church's belief in the "resurrection of the body" was a bit of a stumbling block for a Gentile culture steeped in Greek thinking. Greek philosophy saw the material world as evil, and the individual's goal in death was to escape the body with the immortal soul and transcend into pure spirit. Many, influenced by this thinking, had a problem with the Divine Word/Jesus (*logos*) becoming flesh.[158] For them, that would have meant Jesus became sinful. This is not biblical, as we saw in chapter two.

God called all of his creation, including the physical, *very good.* In the same way, these Greek thinkers could not understand why God would raise *our bodies* from the dead. Besides, wouldn't the body be decayed by Resurrection Day? Because they started from the wrong premise, they began to ask the wrong questions. Paul reiterates their questions—*"How will the dead be raised? What kind*

---

[156] 1 Cor. 15:23, NLT.

[157] 1 Cor. 15:26–27, NLT.

[158] John 1:1–5 and 14.

of bodies will they have?"—to which Paul replied, *"What a foolish question!"*[159] Paul's questioners were asking questions like, "How can one believe in the resurrection of the body? What happens if a cannibal eats a person, and then a shark eats that cannibal, and then the shark gets washed up on the shore and is eaten by birds? How is God going to sort all of that out at the resurrection?"

Paul answers these questions by saying, "You don't understand what you are talking about. First of all, we are discussing a work of God, and secondly, it is not our current bodies that we get back, but new ones." We don't need to preserve our bodies as the Egyptians tried. We are talking about something very different.

So what *does* the Bible teach regarding the resurrection? To answer this, we are going to walk through 1 Corinthians 15:36–52. Before reading the rest of this chapter, read these verses in your Bible.

1 Corinthians 15:36–41

Paul begins to answer this question about the resurrection by giving the example of a seed and a plant. If a plant or a shaft of wheat is going to grow, it must first be buried in the ground.[160] This buried seed then sprouts new life, and what comes out of the ground is something different from the seed that was planted. Paul says that, "in the same way," when people die, they become like seeds that, when resurrected, are going to be given new bodies different from the old body—to which many of us say *Hallelujah*!

Paul continues by stating there are different kinds of bodies, and that not all flesh is the same. To suit different environments, God has created different bodies. A fish has a different body than a bird, just as a bird has a different body than a mammal or a human. "In the same way," God has designed heavenly bodies

---

[159] 1 Cor. 15:35–36, NLT.

[160] Remember, this is an analogy and not to be taken as a doctrinal statement on burial practices. Someone whose body does not get *buried in the ground* is not going to miss the resurrection!

different from earthly bodies. Angels, Cherubim, and Seraphim have bodies different from the ones we have. *There are bodies in the heavens, and there are bodies on earth. The glory of the heavenly bodies is different from the beauty of the earthly bodies.*[161]

1 Corinthians 15:42–44

The bodies we currently possess are perishable, but the new bodies we are going to get are imperishable. Our bodies suffer, feel pain, decay, break down, and eventually die.

This is not the way God originally created us, as we saw earlier, but this has happened because of humanity's rebellion against God in Adam. This disconnected God's creation from the life-giving Creator and brought death. The price tag of sin is death,[162] just as God told Adam and Eve: *"You may freely eat any fruit in the garden except fruit from the tree of the knowledge of good and evil. If you eat of its fruit, you will surely die."*[163] Adam and Eve did disobey God and set the world on a course towards death. Our bodies fall apart, our thoughts are impure, and our motivation is often selfish. We are born on a path heading for self-destruction.[164] These natural bodies of ours are perishable; they have been sown in dishonour and weakness.

Much of this has been talked about already in this book, along with the good news that Christ has conquered this problem of sin and death, promising those who follow him forgiveness and new life. A new life that will result in new bodies—bodies that will be imperishable and raised in glory and power! For this reason, the Christian can say, "I believe in the life everlasting."

So, what is this new body going to be like? The Bible doesn't talk about the dead as disembodied souls. This idea also has its origins in Greek philosophy, and has mistakenly been accepted by a

---

[161] 1 Cor. 15:40, NLT.

[162] Rom. 6:23.

[163] Gen. 2:16b–17, NLT.

[164] Ps. 51:5.

number of Christians. The word "soul," in the Bible, simply means, "living being." When God created Adam's flesh "from the dust of the ground," he was not alive. God breathed his spirit[165] into Adam, and he became "a living being"—a soul. Adam's soul did not pre-exist, but came into being when God's spirit joined Adam's flesh.

The soul is our personhood, not a ghost trapped inside our body. A body cannot live without a soul, nor can a soul live without a body. The resurrection is not only a bodily resurrection. If this were the case, then death is not really a conscious death, but only a bodily death, with the soul living in a different state.

This creates all kinds of theological problems. For instance, this would indicate that only the body was sinful and in need of a death and a resurrection. The fact is, our entire beings (our souls) have been affected by sin and are in danger of eternal death. The miracle of what Christ has done is not that we never really die, but live as disembodied souls until we get a new body. The miracle is that, although we actually and truly die, we really come back to life again!

The resurrection *of the body* is a bit misleading. It was empha-sized in the creed to counter those who did not believe in a *bodily* resurrection, but some have now interpreted it as speaking of ***only a bodily*** resurrection. They claim the soul never dies, but lives and awaits the resurrection of the body. This is contrary to the many passages in the Bible that speak of resurrection day as the day Christ comes again and brings the *dead* back to life—he does not just give the already living new bodies.

When the creed says "the resurrection of the body," it is totally correct, but in accordance with the teaching of Scripture, we must remember that this bodily resurrection occurs on the day the dead come back to life, and does not just refer to our outer shell. We die with natural bodies and are brought back from the dead with spiritual bodies.

---

165 This is God's life source, not the Holy Spirit.

1 Corinthians 15:44–50

In answering more specifically what these new bodies will be like, Paul writes, *Every human being has an earthly body just like Adam's, but our heavenly bodies will be just like Christ's.*[166]

When Jesus died on the cross, it was not only his flesh that died, but every part of him. To say only Jesus' flesh died would be to say only his body was needed to take away the world's sin. It would also say that Jesus never really died, but simply existed without a body for three days. The miracle of what happened in Christ, however, was that he truly died, but defeated death by actually coming to life again.

Warren Wiersbe reminds us of this when he writes, "On the cross, our Lord suffered and died. His body was put to death, and his spirit died when he was made sin."[167]

Jesus' new body, after his resurrection, was tangible. He could eat, and pick things up, and he even said to his disciples, *"Look at me, I am not a ghost."*[168] At the same time, however, Jesus could suddenly appear and disappear at different locations.[169] Jesus had a new, imperishable body raised in glory and power. Paul compares our new resurrected bodies to Christ's. Christians will be raised with bodies in the likeness of Christ's body after his resurrection.

1 Corinthians 15:51–52 and 1 Thessalonians 4:13–16

Christians are those who have accepted what Christ has done for them and, therefore, they are declared righteous. Christians, however, still struggle with their old nature. This is what some

---

[166] 1 Cor. 15:48, NLT.

[167] Warren Wiersbe, *1 Peter—Be Hopeful* (Wheaton, IL: Victor, 1982) p. 91.

[168] Luke 24:37–43.

[169] Luke 24:28–31.

theologians call the "already, but not yet" reality of Christianity. A Christian is saved from their sin and raised to new life *now*, but at the same time, they await their salvation and resurrection—which only comes *after* they have physically died and been given new life. The Bible describes the Holy Spirit as given to the Christian as a deposit, guaranteeing what is to come.[170]

According to the verses in the heading of this section, when Christians die, they await the last trumpet. The last trumpet will sound at that moment in history chosen by God when Christ comes again. At that time, the dead in Christ will be raised to life with a spiritual body similar to the kind Jesus had after his resurrection.

This has caused some to speculate about what happens between their death and their resurrection at the Second Coming of Christ. They may ask, "Is there not a verse that teaches us that absence from the body is presence with the Lord?"[171] What about Jesus' words to the thief on the cross when he told him that he would be with Jesus in paradise *today*?[172]

Let's remember—these verses cannot be looked at in isolation from the rest of Scripture, but neither can we ignore them. Luke 23:43 and 2 Corinthians 5:8 need to be read alongside of 1 Corinthians 15:51–52 and 1 Thessalonians 4:13–16, and 1 Corinthians 15:51–52 and 1 Thessalonians 4:13–16 need to acknowledge Luke 23:43 and 2 Corinthians 5:8. Is there a way they can fit together? I believe there is.

The answer comes when we understand time from God's dimension, rather than ours. Paul often refers to the intermediate state as "sleep," but this is simply an example. We don't actually lie down for a nap in some cosmic nursery until Resurrection Day! What Paul is alluding to, however, is a time of unconsciousness. For the "sleeping" individual, time really ceases to exist. In the dead state,

---

170 Eph. 1:14.

171 2 Cor. 5:8.

172 Luke 23:43.

this person is outside of time. Two hundred years from one person's death to his or her resurrection, and another person's five hundred years simply do not exist for them. Let me give you an example.

Let's say you are watching a movie on your DVD player, and at some point during the show, you decide to get a snack from the fridge. As you get up, you *pause* the movie and go and make your snack. After ten minutes, you come back and continue watching the movie. When you *un-pause* the DVD, not a single moment of time has elapsed for the movie, although for you ten minutes passed.

In the same way, death means the separation of our spirit (God's life source) from our bodies. When this happens, we, as living beings (souls), cease to exist. The miracle is that, because we serve the one who conquered death, this ceasing to exist will only be a state of "pause." We believe in the same God that Abraham believed in. *The God who brings the dead back to life and who brings into existence what didn't exist before.*[173] Anthony Thiselton, professor of Biblical Studies at the University of Nottingham, England, describes it this way:

> The Bible raises no difficulty. Quite clearly from the point of view of experience, the dead believer is conscious of no interval between dying and entering the fullness of the presence of Christ. Yet equally clearly, the final judgment and resurrection do not take place at one time for one individual and another time for another; they are single events for the whole community.... It is difficult for us to appreciate events outside time.[174]

Individuals who have given their lives over to Christ can say yes, the very *moment,* on the *today* of their death, they will see Christ immediately from their existential perspective. Historically, however, each individual's personal *today* will happen on the specific day in history when the last trumpet blasts!

---

[173] Rom. 4:17, NLT.

[174] Robin Keeley, Ed., *Exploring Christian Faith* (Nashville, TN: Nelson, 1982) p. 284; Anthony Thiselton, "Destiny."

The Bible sees people as whole beings. When humanity fell from God, it was a spiritual, physical, emotional, intellectual, and relational death. Christ, however, brought life back to all areas of our being. Ultimately, he is the only one who can heal us, spiritually, physically, emotionally, intellectually, and relationally. He is the only one who can make us truly human once again!

When we surrender our lives to him, we are given the hope and promise of new life in all areas of our being. On that *day* in history, which is experienced on the *day* of our death, we will be like Jesus—the truly human one. We will live forever as imperishable, immortal living beings (souls)—with new bodies, and with God's spirit flowing through us!

1 Corinthians 15:53–55

For our perishable earthly bodies must be transformed into heavenly bodies that will never die. When this happens—when our perishable earthly bodies have been transformed into heavenly bodies that will never die—then, at last, the Scriptures will come true: *"Death is swallowed up in victory. O death, where is your victory? O death, where is your sting?"*[175]

A Closing Story

One day, a man was walking through a graveyard and noticed a tombstone with the following epitaph:

"Pause my friend, as you walk by,
As you are now so was I.
As I am now, so you will be,
Prepare, my friend, to follow me."

Suddenly he spotted some other words carved into the corner of the tombstone. They read:

---

[175] 1 Cor. 15:53–55, NIV.

"To follow you is not my intent,
Until I know which way you went!"

I believe in the resurrection of the dead and the life everlasting, Amen!

conclusion

On one of Paul's missionary journeys, he arrived in the city of Thessalonica.

As was Paul's custom, he went to the synagogue service, and for three Sabbaths in a row he interpreted the Scriptures to the people. He was explaining and proving the prophecies about the sufferings of the Messiah and his rising from the dead.[176]

When Paul arrived in the city of Berea, he did the same thing, *as was his custom*. Notice, however, the response of the Bereans:

And the people of Berea were more open-minded than those in Thessalonica, and they listened eagerly to Paul's message. They searched the Scriptures day after day to check up on Paul and Silas, to see if they were really teaching the truth.[177]

[176] Acts 17:2–3, NLT.
[177] Acts 17:11, NLT.

What a wonderful lesson from a noble people. The people of Berea neither shut out the message before they heard it, nor just blindly accepted it. Instead, they *searched* the Scriptures, to see if what they were being taught was true. Then came the point where they had to make a decision for or against.

My prayer for you, whether you are a Christian or not, is that you will model your life after the Bereans. May this book you just read only be a step along your journey.

Ladd, George E. *A Theology of the New Testament*. Grand Rapids, MI: Eerdmans, 1974.

McDowell, Josh. *Evidence That Demands a Verdict*. San Bernardino, CA: Nelson, 1972.

Morgan, Robert J. *On This Day*. Nashville, TN: Thomas Nelson, 1997.

Peterson, Eugene. *Five Smooth Stones*. Grand Rapids, MI: Eerdmans, 1980.

Posterski, Donald. *True To You*. Winfield, BC: Wood Lake, 1995.

Russell, Bertrand. *Why I am Not a Christian*. New York, NY: Touchstone, 1957.

Spurgeon, Charles. *Lectures to My Students*. Lynchburg, Virginia: The Old Time Gospel Hour, 1894.

Stott, John. *Christian Mission*. Downers Grove, IL: IVP, 1975.

Tacitus, *Annals*, XV, #44

Wiersbe, Warren. *1 Peter—Be Hopeful*. Wheaton, IL: Victor, 1982.

Holy Bible, New Living Translation, copyright © 1996 by Tyndale Charitable Trust.

bibliography

Akers, John N., John H. Armstrong, and John D. Woodbridge, (Eds). *This We Believe.* Grand Rapids, MI: Zondervan, 2000.

Behe, Michael. *Darwin's Black Box.* New York, NY: Simon & Schuster, 1996.

Bibby, Reginald, *Fragmented Gods.* Toronto, ON: Irwin, 1987.

Bibby, Reginald. *Restless Gods.* Toronto, ON: Stoddart, 2002.

Chesterton, G.K. *Heretics/Orthodoxy.* Nashville, TN: Nelson, 2000.

France, Dick. *Exploring The Christian Faith.* Nashville. TN: Thomas Nelson, 1996.

Green, Michael. *World on the Run.* Leicester, England: Inter-Varsity, 1983.

Guinness, Os. (Ed). *Steering Through Chaos.* Colorado Springs, CO: NavPress, 2000.

Harrison, Everett F. *A Short Life of Christ.* Grand Rapids, MI: Eerdmans, 1968.

Johnson, Philip. *Darwin on Trial.* Downers Grove, IL: IVP, 1991.

Keeley, Robin. (Ed). *Exploring Christian Faith.* Nashville, TN: Nelson, 1982.